10-00

STUDIES IN TUDOR AND STUART LITERATURE

General Editors

F.H. MARES *and* A.T. BRISSENDEN

Anthony Munday

THE ENGLISH ROMAN LIFE

Edited by

PHILIP J. AYRES

CLARENDON PRESS · OXFORD

1980

Oxford University Press, Walton Street, Oxford OX2 6DP

OXFORD LONDON GLASGOW
NEW YORK TORONTO MELBOURNE WELLINGTON
KUALA LUMPUR SINGAPORE JAKARTA HONG KONG TOKYO
DELHI BOMBAY CALCUTTA MADRAS KARACHI
NAIROBI DAR ES SALAAM CAPE TOWN

Published in the United States by
Oxford University Press, New York

© *Philip J. Ayres 1980*

British Library Cataloguing in Publication Data

Munday, Anthony
   The English Roman Life. — (Studies in Tudor and Stuart Literature).
   1. English College, *Rome* — History
   I. Title
   II. Ayres, Philip J   III. Series
   207′.45′632   BX920.R/   79-40268

ISBN 0-19-812635-2

Typesetting by Hope Services, Abingdon, Oxon
Printed in Great Britain by
Billing & Sons Ltd., Guildford and Worcester

for

MY PARENTS

PREFACE

This is the third volume in the series of Studies in Tudor and Stuart Literature, the aim of which is to make available a number of works of the sixteenth and seventeenth centuries which are of interest for their literary or historic value, or as documents in the history of taste and culture. The texts are established from the examination of early editions and manuscripts, taking into account the work of previous editors where necessary. The introduction sets the work in its social and literary context, discussing the author in his time, the work itself, and the treatment of the text. Annotations are intended to elucidate difficult passages, discuss usage, comment on textual problems, and refer the reader to other editions and relevant material.

The initial research leading to the publication of the series was supported by the Australian Research Grants Committee, and, as general editors, we gratefully acknowledge this assistance. We are also happy to thank Miss Robin Eaden for her help in checking information and proofs.

Department of English   F. H. MARES
University of Adelaide   A. T. BRISSENDEN

ACKNOWLEDGMENTS

In preparing this edition of *The English Roman Life* I have been helped in numerous ways by a variety of people. Much of the work was carried out in the Rare Books Room of the University Library in Cambridge during 1976, and I am indebted to the librarians for facilitating my work there and to the Council of Monash University for providing me with the period of study leave I needed to complete the book. Gail Ward typed the final manuscript and I thank her for her care and patience. My greatest debt is to the General Editors, Mr. F. H. Mares and Dr. Alan Brissenden. The scrupulous attention they gave to the early drafts resulted in criticism and suggestions that were invariably helpful. They also gave that less tangible but so necessary thing, encouragement.

PHILIP J. AYRES

CONTENTS

PLATES

These are reproduced by courtesy of
the Bodleian Library.

ABBREVIATIONS AND SHORT TITLES
USED IN THE NOTES

1	*The English Romayne Lyfe ... London ... 1582.*
2	*The English Romayne Lyfe ... London ... 1590.*
A.P.C.	*Acts of the Privy Council.*
C.R.S.	*Catholic Record Society.*
C.S.P.Dom.	*Calendar of State Papers; Domestic* (volume indicated by the years covered).
The Copy	*The Copie of a Double Letter ... containing ... the cause, and maner of the death, of one Richard Atkins, executed by fire in Rome, the seconde of August 1581* [Rouen?, 1581?] .
D.N.B.	*The Dictionary of National Biography.*
Discovery	*A Discouerie of Edmund Campion and his Confederates ... London ... 1582.*
E.R.L.	*The English Roman Life.*
Haddock	Richard Haddock's letter to William Allen, dated 9 March 1579, in M. A. Tierney, ed., *Dodd's Church History of England*, Vol. ii (London, 1839), Appendix, pp. cccl-ccclxi.
Liber Ruber	*Liber Ruber Venerabilis Collegii Anglorum de Urbe*, ed. W. Kelly, in *Catholic Record Society*, xxxvii (London, 1940), 9 ff.
O.E.D.	*The Oxford English Dictionary.*
Palladio	Andrea Palladio, *Descritione de le chiese de Roma* (Rome, 1554).
s.n.	side-note.
Tilley	M. P. Tilley, *A Dictionary of the Proverbs in England in the Sixteenth and Seventeenth Centuries* (Ann Arbor, 1950).

INTRODUCTION

1. *The Background*

Anthony Munday was a versatile and copious author. He was playwright, translator of continental romances, writer of prose fiction, balladeer, news reporter in the Protestant cause, chronicler, and deviser of pageants for the City of London. Among much that is mediocre he produced one book, *The English Roman Life* (1582), which is not only very readable today but has value both as a historical document and as travel literature. The background to its composition, though it reflects unfavourably on Munday's character, takes nothing from the book's worth in these respects.

The precise date of his birth is unknown, but it is now clear that Munday was born some time in 1560—quite probably a few days before his baptism on 13 October 1560. He was buried on 9 August 1633, an old man but not the man of eighty that his tombstone, quoted in the 1633 edition of John Stow's *Survey of London*, reported him to have been.[1] His father Christopher Munday, a freeman of the Draper's Company who worked, however, as a stationer, and his mother Jane both died early.[2] In 1576 the orphaned Anthony became an apprentice to the stationer John Allde, in whose employ he remained until 1578 when, probably in the autumn, his indentures were cancelled on his own request to allow him to travel abroad.[3]

---

[1] The relevant documents were produced, independently, by Leslie Hotson, 'Anthony Mundy's Birth-date', *Notes and Queries*, cciv (1959), 2-4; and Mark Eccles, 'Anthony Munday', *Studies in The English Renaissance Drama*, ed. J. W. Bennett et al. (New York, 1959), pp. 95-105. Although his name is sometimes spelt *Mundy* by scholars, he himself spells it *Munday* at the end of both the Dedication and the note "To the . . . reader." This is also the form used in the *D.N.B.*

[2] Eccles, p. 98.

[3] See Celeste Turner, *Anthony Mundy, an Elizabethan Man of Letters* (Berkeley, 1928), pp. 13-16. On the date of Munday's journey, as on a number of other points, the entry in the *D.N.B.* is unreliable.

The motive behind his trip to Rome, which he was to describe so vividly four years later, is unclear. His biographer, Celeste Turner (Wright), argues that he went as a recent convert to Catholicism. But her claim—an old one—that his patron the Earl of Oxford, to whom Munday had just dedicated at the remarkably young age of seventeen his translation of the now lost *Galien of France*, was a secret Catholic rests on no sound evidence at all; while her argument that both Munday's employer John Allde and John Charlewood, who printed a number of Munday's early books, were probably Catholics too is based on nothing but rather flimsy circumstantial evidence.[4] The journey can be accounted for on other, more likely, grounds. There is no evidence that Munday was ever a Catholic and a good deal in *The English Roman Life* to suggest that he was not, including his adoption of an alias. He claimed in the dedication of *The Mirror of Mutability* (1579) that the Earl of Oxford had encouraged the journey as a way of attaining 'some understanding of the languages' (apparently *Galien of France* could have been better 'Englished' than it was). In *The English Roman Life* itself Munday mentions that the reason for his trip was nothing more than his 'desire to see strange countries, as also affection to learn the languages' (ll. 84-5). In those few words surely lies both the reason and the excuse, in that order, while boredom with his life as an apprentice no doubt provided the spur. Certainly wanderlust is a far more satisfactory explanation for his travelling abroad than piety, or another that has been suggested—that he had the future *English Roman Life* in mind (a costly way of getting material).[5]

[4] See Turner, pp. 10 ff., and the same author's 'Young Anthony Mundy Again', *Studies in Philology*, lvi (1959), 154 ff. (published under her married name, Celeste Turner Wright).

[5] This motive was suggested by Beatrice H. Thompson, 'Anthony Munday's Journey to Rome', *Durham University Journal*, xxiv (1941), 4, and is well answered by Guiseppe Galigani, 'La "English Romayne Lyfe" di A. Mundy', *Rivista di letterature moderne e comparate* (Florence), xviii (1965), 112. Little credence attaches to Munday's claim at the trial of Edmund Campion and other priests in 1581, that he went to 'undermine them and sift out their purposes'—Richard Simpson, *Edmund Campion* (London, 1867), p. 305—although it is just possible that he was asked informally by someone in author-

It is curiously appropriate that his companion should have been Thomas Nowell. In *The English Roman Life* Munday makes much of Nowell's Catholic sympathies, and indeed Nowell was still in the English College in Rome in 1582 when the book appeared. None of the scholars who have examined this work and related published documents seem to have noticed, though, that in 1583 Nowell was dismissed from the College as unsuitable for the priesthood and that he subsequently became a spy against Catholics in England (see l. 92, note). By a cruel irony, his 'Catholicism' was to be perpetuated in the 1590 edition, in which not one of Munday's aspersions on the unfortunate Nowell's religious inclinations was deleted.

As Munday later revealed, it was with the help of Catholics that he and Nowell reached Rome—via Amiens, Paris, Lyons, and Milan—on 1 February 1579, and it was with Catholic help that they were able to stay in Rome at so little expense to themselves, in the English College, newly established as a seminary. Munday could hardly have chosen a better time to visit the city and the College. He was able to see the Carnival, the catacombs had just been rediscovered, and the English College was about to suffer the most dramatic changes in its history with the rebellion of its English students against their rector. Fortunately Munday had the eye of a social historian and a memory for fine detail. The things he chose to remember most clearly and to record over three years later have both interest and significance, and the prose in which they were recorded gives them life.

After a little more than three months in the city, most of that time as a guest and then a student in the College, Munday left Rome and was in London again before 23 July, when *The Admirable Deliverance of 266 Christians by J. Reynard* (J. Fox), to which he contributed some verses, was licensed.[6] A variety of books followed—prose fiction in the shape of *Zelauto* (1580), ballads, sensational news,

---

ity to take particular note of the doings of any English Catholic exiles he might come across.

    [6] Turner, p. 24. In these verses Munday claims, falsely, to have met Fox in Rome in 1577.

and attacks on the theatre—until in 1581 there appeared his *Brief Discourse of the Taking of Edmund Campion*, licensed on 24 July. Campion and Robert Persons had arrived in England in June 1580 on the first Jesuit mission to England. With them were a number of young priests from the English College in Rome.

No doubt the need for money, and the certainty that such material was particularly saleable, provided Munday with more than enough motivation to become an anti-Catholic reporter and milk his Roman trip dry.[7] Fear probably provided a secondary motive. He had stayed at the English College under another name, but he may still have felt insecure. Should the fact of his stay there by some chance become known, the worst would be assumed. Generally, anti-Catholic feeling was intensifying, particularly since the arrival of the Jesuit mission.[8] If, on the other hand, Munday were to prove his patriotic credentials, the stay in Rome might even be turned to his advantage.

The motive of fear, the precarious nature of the literary profession, and the fact of his youth go some way towards making his subsequent treachery against former friends understandable. It should also be conceded that, in the climate of opinion prevailing at the time, Munday may have become a sincere, even a zealous, anti-papist. That he continued his 'patriotic' activities at least as late as 1612, formalizing them from 1588 or earlier in his official role of government messenger and hunter of recusants under Richard Topcliffe, and that he hunted puritans during the Marprelate controversy are facts that do not by themselves dispose of an originally 'sincere' motivation. Once in the employ of a secret service it is often hard to get out. That said, it has to be admitted that he did as much to blacken his name as did his enemies. Francis Meres was surely referring to more than plays when, in the *Palladis Tamia* (1598), he commended Munday as 'our best plotter', and with

[7] Munday found the literary profession as precarious as anyone else at this time. See, e.g., E. H. Miller, *The Professional Writer in Elizabethan England* (Cambridge, Mass., 1959), pp. 211-12, 214-15.

[8] These facts are rightly emphasized by Celeste Turner Wright, 'Young Anthony Mundy Again', p. 157.

good reason, although some contemporaries would have
detected irony in the word 'best'. Richard Simpson quotes
from an official report of 1590 on Munday's way with
recusants:

> He hath been in divers places where I have passed; whose dealing
> hath been very rigorous, and yet done very small good, but rather
> much hurt; for in one place, under pretence to seek for *Agnus Deis*
> and hallowed grains, he carried from a widow 40 *l.*, the which he
> took out of a chest. A few of these matches will either raise a rebel-
> lion, or cause your officers to be murdered.[9]

Whatever his initial motivation may have been, he wasted
no time, for the *Brief Discourse* was licensed within forty-
eight hours of Campion's arrival under guard in London.
Rushing into print, Munday gave himself no time to check
his facts, and his account was quickly contradicted by
George Elliot, a former Catholic and the man chiefly
responsible for Campion's capture, in Elliot's *A Very True
Report of the Apprehension of E. Campion* (1581)—'a
controlment of a most untrue former book set out by one
A.M., alias Anthony Munday', as the title-page had it. Also
quickly contradicted about this time, again by an equally
anti-Catholic account, was Munday's *Arraignment and
Execution of . . . E. Duckett, alias Haunce* (1581), which
drew forth *A True Report of the Arraignment and Execution of the Late Popish Traitor E. Haunce* (1581).

Naturally, many people, Protestants included, thought
Munday a singularly unreliable witness when he and others
appeared on 20 November 1581 to testify against certain
priests he had met—Henry Orton at Lyons, and Ralph
Sherwin, Luke Kirby, and Edward Rishton in Rome—and
against others, including Campion, he had never seen

---

[9] *Edmund Campion*, p. 312. A colleague, Mr. Ian Laurenson, has drawn
my attention to an epigram by Sir John Davies, probably composed earlier
than November 1594, which is very revealing:
> In Mundayum.
> Munday I sweare shalbee a hollidaye,
>   If hee forsweare himselfe but once a daye.
See *The Poems of Sir John Davies*, ed. Robert Krueger (Oxford, 1975), p. 157.
That this epigram concerns Munday seems highly likely, especially in view of
another in this collection titled 'In Bretton' which appears to refer to Nicholas
Breton.

before. Munday's court-room revelations of their 'treasons' were reported in his *Discovery of Edmund Campion and his Confederates* (1582), printed shortly after the executions of Campion, Sherwin, and Alexander Briant (1 December 1581), which he describes in vivid detail. What he had to reveal did not even amount to convincing circumstantial evidence; all he could report were various irreverent comments on Elizabeth and her ministers that he had heard in France and Italy, rumours about invasions, and hopes for a restoration of Catholicism in England—all soon to be set out in *The English Roman Life*. He subsequently did his reputation further harm in his *Brief and True Report of the Execution of Certain Traitors* (1582) by reporting, without contradicting, Luke Kirby's claim that he had gone out of his way to befriend Munday, assisting him in Rome 'out of his own purse' even though he knew Munday was not a Catholic. Clearly, the betrayal of former friends, providing they were Catholics, was to Munday no treachery at all. His Protestant readers would understand.

The Catholic *True Report of the Death ... of M. Campion Jesuit* (Douai, early 1582) was an answer to Munday's *Discovery of Edmund Campion* (on the title-page of which Munday had claimed to have once been 'the Pope's scholar' in the English College, Rome), and it very effectively attacked his credibility. Its 'caveat to the reader touching A. M. his discovery' deserves to be quoted at some length.

Munday, who was first a stage player (no doubt a calling of some credit), after an apprentice which time he well served with deceiving of his master, then wandering towards Italy, by his own report became a cozener in his journey. Coming to Rome, in his short abode there, was charitably relieved, but never admitted in the seminary as he pleaseth to lie in the title of his book, and being weary of well doing, returned home to his first vomit again. I omit to declare how this scholar new come out of Italy did play extempore, those gentlemen and others which were present can best give witness of his dexterity, who being weary of his folly, hissed him from his stage. Then being thereby discouraged, he set forth a ballad against plays, but yet (O constant youth) he now begins again to ruffle upon the stage. I omit among other places his behaviour in Barbican with his good mistress, and mother . . . . Yet I think it not amiss to remember thee of this boy's infelicity two several ways of late notorious. First he writing upon the death of Everard Haunce, was immediately controlled and disproved by one of his own hatch, and shortly after setting forth the apprehension of M. Campion, was disproved by George (I was about to say) Judas Elliott, who writing against him, proved that those things he did were for very lucre's sake only, and not for the truth, although he himself be a person of the same predicament, of whom I must say, that if felony be honesty, then he may for his behaviour be taken for a lawful witness against so good men.

Two of these points could be answered. The 'deceiving of his master' is refuted by a glowing testimonial from John Allde printed in Munday's reply, *A Brief Answer Made unto Two Seditious Pamphlets* (1582), which incidentally revealed that Munday and Elliott had resolved their quarrel. And Munday had of course been admitted into the English College (a fact testified to by another note, secured from Luke Kirby some time before Kirby's execution and also printed in the *Brief Answer*), but not under his own name. Since his mother was dead and the first of Munday's five children was born on 28 June 1584, it has been suggested that the word 'mother' in the reference to 'his behaviour in Barbican with his good mistress, and mother' may mean 'mother-in-law'.[10] Whatever the implication was, Munday chose to ignore it. The rest, including the report of Munday's curiously inconstant relationship with the stage, was presumably unanswerable.[11]

The English Roman Life, which appeared next, was Munday's final reply to his enemies. Here he would prove, to those who remained unconvinced, that he had indeed been to Rome, that he had been admitted into the English College there, and that everywhere he had heard treason spoken and plotted against England and her queen.

2. *The Work*

As a historical document *The English Roman Life* has two distinct claims to importance. It offers historians of English Catholicism a unique and detailed record of daily life in

[10] See Eccles, 'Anthony Munday', pp. 98-9.
[11] In 1582 Stephen Gosson, in *Plays Confuted in Five Actions*, used similar terms in attacking a playwright, presumably Munday, who after forsaking the stage 'turned himself like the dog to his vomit, to plays again' (G3^V).

the English College in Rome at that time, and a participant's account of a crucial episode in the College's development, the successful rebellion early in 1579 of the English students against their Welsh rector Maurice Clenocke ('Doctor Morris' as Munday calls him) and the institution, at their request, of Jesuit control. Its value in terms of Roman social history is also high; although Munday tells us little of Rome that we cannot discover from other sources, the significance of his account is that it is first hand; that it dwells, understandably, on those less savoury aspects of the city that the contemporary guide-books shy away from; that its descriptions are so precise and readable; and that, being all this, it is at the same time generally reliable in terms of the facts it presents, though of course the interpretation is always open to question.

This general reliability is established by the many events and details in the book which can be verified by independent documents. Verification is particularly desirable in this case, given Munday's activities from 1581 and his proven reputation for deceit. His stay at the College is proved not only by his detailed description of life in that institution but by several documents dating from the early months of 1579. The papers of Cardinal Morone, the Protector of England who figures prominently in *The English Roman Life*, were discovered in the Vatican Library around 1962 and, as Anthony Kenny has revealed, they contain two lists of students in the English College.[12] These are earlier than the *Liber Ruber*, the College diary in which Thomas Nowell's name (but not Munday's) appears, and date from early 1579—no later than mid-March. They establish, together and in relation to other documents previously available, that Munday and Nowell were living in the College early in 1579 (according to *The English Roman Life* they arrived in Rome on 1 February) and that Munday's alias was, in its Latinized form, 'Antonius Auleus' (perhaps Hawley—see l. 477, note). Munday and Nowell are referred to as 'humanistae'—grammar students. Kenny also quotes a letter, from among the same papers, to

[12] Cited as documents Vat. Lat. 12159, 123 and 12159, 201, by Kenny, 'Antony Munday in Rome', *Recusant History*, vi (1962), 158-62.

Morone from Owen Lewis dated 28 March 1579, three and a half weeks after the rebellion had come to a head. Owen Lewis, who has his place in Munday's book, was a close friend of Maurice Clenocke's and had no reason to like Munday: 'I request that your Eminence give instruction that Thomas, a Welsh boy of seventeen years, of very promising character and more learned (as I hear) than those two grammarians who lately intruded themselves into the register of students to make up the number in the presence of his Holiness, be admitted as a student of the seminary.'[13] There can be no doubt that Munday and Nowell were 'those two grammarians'. Further proof that they accompanied the thirty-three English students who left the College on 4 March 1579 and that they were present at the subsequent audience with Pope Gregory XIII is provided by the closeness of Munday's account to that of Richard Haddock, a student in the College at the time, and by a letter from Robert Persons to William Goode in which Persons describes at length the causes and consequences of the troubles in the College. Extracts from these letters are provided in the Appendix at the end of this volume.

Munday and Nowell could stay in the College for eight days as pilgrims to the city but in fact stayed longer, despite the objection of 'Doctor Morris' and the increasing inconvenience to which Munday at least was put (see in particular ll. 2251 ff.). The support of the English students must have been vital. Once Maurice Clenocke had been removed from the rectorship Munday and his friend were able to stay on as students, presumably after expressing the intention to take the missionary oath.[14] He and Nowell avoided taking it on 23 April, but Nowell's name was included in the official *Liber Ruber* on 29 April, whereas 'Auleus' was not.[15] This suggests that Munday had left the College by the end of April. He probably began his homeward journey soon after, perhaps with the priest Askew, who left in May;[16] the

[13] Translated by Kenny, p. 161, and cited as Vat. Lat. 12159, 152.
[14] Kenny, p. 161, and Galigani, p. 116.
[15] *Liber Ruber*, p. 13, item 51.
[16] According to the *Douay Diaries* (*Records of the English Catholics under the Penal Laws*), ed. T. F. Knox (London, 1878), p. 154, cited by Kenny,

intervening days could have been spent travelling to and from Naples, which Munday claimed to have visited.[17]

The two and a half months he spent in this fairly small institution (there were forty students there when he arrived) are more than enough to guarantee the accuracy of Munday's description of the life within it, a life that must have offered him many inducements to remain there, not the least of them being the cuisine:

> As for their fare, trust me it is very fine and delicate, for every man hath his own trencher, his manchet, knife, spoon and fork laid by it, and then a fair white napkin covering it, with his glass and pot of wine set by him. And the first mess, or *antepast* as they call it, that is brought to the table is some fine meat to urge them have an appetite: as sometime the Spanish anchovies, and sometime stewed prunes and raisins of the sun together, having such fine tart syrup made to them as I promise you a weak stomach would very well digest them. . . . The fifth and last is sometime cheese, sometime preserved conceits, sometime figs, almonds and raisins, a lemon and sugar, a pomegranate, or some such sweet gear: for they know that Englishmen loveth sweetmeats. (ll. 1094–1121)

Although discipline is strictly enforced and each day is highly organized, it is noticeable that there is mutual respect within the discipline—the English–Welsh issue aside—and within the organization a civilized regard for leisure and amusement.

Munday's descriptions reveal a close attention to items that may at first seem trivial but which often serve to create atmosphere. In the passage just quoted, for example, Munday 'sets the table' before he describes the food, so that the reader in a sense partakes of the meal. Similarly in the following lines it is the fire and the fact of winter that turn what might otherwise have been just another item of 'treason' into an occasion:

> After supper, if it be in winter-time, they go with the Jesuits and sit about a great fire talking, and in all their talk they strive who shall speak worst of Her Majesty, of some of her Council, of some bishop

---

p. 161, Askew arrived at the College of Douai (Reims) on 9 July 1579, from Rome via Paris, accompanied by a certain 'Antonius' who left for England a few days later. The *Liber Ruber* establishes that Askew left Rome in May.

[17] See the dedication of *The Mirror of Mutability* (1579), from which it is also clear that he visited Venice and Padua on his way home.

here, or suchlike: so that the Jesuits themselves will often take up their hands and bless themselves, to hear what abominable tales they will tell them.   (ll. 1153–60)

This attention to details which are so often purely incidental is a feature of Munday's prose style rather than the result of an attempt to convince the sceptical that he witnessed what he describes. The prose itself is sometimes flawed in its syntax, and Munday's vocabulary is not always taxed very far. Almost everything about the Priscilla catacomb, for example, is 'great':

. . . through the great report they made of this vault, one of the priests, two of the scholars and I, took with us a line, and two or three great lights, and so we went to this aforesaid vault; we going along in farther and farther, there we saw certain places one above another, three and three on either side, during a great way in length: and these, places they said to be some of them the graves of persecuted saints and martyrs.   (ll. 1898–1907)

But the size of the torches and the depth of the catacomb are at least noticed, as are the number and status of the visitors, their 'line', and the sense of movement ('farther and farther'). Everything contributes to a feeling of awe and mystery. When Munday turns his attention to the Jewish ghetto, the reception of Jewish converts in St. John Lateran on Holy Saturday, the Roman Carnival, or the confraternities of *Disciplinati*, each is precisely visualized. The description of the carnival (ll. 2683–2751), with its lavish costumes, disguises, vendettas, bustling crowds, noise, and general debauchery, is particularly graphic, Munday's predilection for things 'great' notwithstanding.

The survey of the churches and their relics, which might easily have made tedious reading, is nicely sceptical and infused with irony ('a company of rotten bones, God knows of what they be', 'a holy relic', 'a singular relic', 'this is no simple relic'). And if Munday is unaware of the faint absurdity of his own pious exclamations ('O horrible and abominable blasphemy') or the hypocrisy of reporting with hardly disguised relish the strongest terms of abuse used against members of Elizabeth's Privy Council and then asking the reader 'to use some reverence in reading these undecent words', he punctures the pretensions of his enemies with wit and style. He is acutely aware of the potentially or actually farcical situation, and some of the best passages are pure farce—the hermit friar living in the catacombs, for instance, or Munday's experience during his period of forced residence in the College store-room next to the 'common house of office' with its 'sweet smell'. The readiness to laugh at himself, here and elsewhere, adds considerably to the appeal of his narrative.

These qualities, and the undoubted historical interest it has for readers today, lift *The English Roman Life* distinctly above the rest of Munday's work. Philip Henslowe appreciated Munday's abilities as a dramatist sufficiently to employ him, alone or in collaboration, on a host of plays from at least 1595 until 1602, and *The Downfall* and *The Death of Robert Earl of Huntington* (both 1601) provide perhaps the best examples of his mature dramatic work. His prose fiction—*Zelauto* (1580), for instance—is very ordinary fare indeed. The City of London saw fit to use his talents as a writer of civic pageants until 1621, although the records of the livery companies show Middleton progressively displacing Munday in the City's favours, while the Ironmongers were so unhappy over the quality of his work in 1609 that they ordered him before their Court to face their complaints.[18] It is probably fair to say that of all the material he produced, *The English Roman Life* is the only book that deserves to be more often read than it is.

3. *The Text*

The basis for the present text is the Henry E. Huntington Library copy of the first edition of 1582 (STC 18272). Four photo-copies of this edition—two in the British Library, one in the Bodleian Library, and the Huntington Library copy—were mechanically collated, minor variants appearing in the inner forme of Sheet B and the outer

---

[18] See the Malone Society *Collections III* (Oxford, 1954), p. 76. Ben Jonson, satirizing Munday as Antonio Balladino in *The Case is Altered* (1599), has a character recognize him as 'Pageant Poet to the City of London' ('when a worse cannot be had'). The same character reminds Antonio that he 'is in print already for the best plotter', an allusion to the Meres reference referred to above.

formes of Sheets D, F, and G. 1582 collates 4°: A–K⁴ L²
(K4 + x1). It was printed by John Charlewood for Nicholas
Ling, having been licensed on 21 June 1582 'under th[e
h] andes of the Bishop of London and Master Dewce' (SR.
II. 413).

A second edition appeared in 1590 (STC 18273), again
printed by Charlewood for Ling. The title-page of 1590 is
set up to resemble that of 1582, though neither this nor
any other area of the text is a line-for-line reprint, since
the 1590 text was set up more economically on nine sheets.
The woodcut illustrations of 1582 (x1 in the collation
above) reappear in 1590, interpolated between I3 and I4.
1590 collates 4°: A–B⁴ C⁴ (± C⁴) D–I⁴ (I3 + x1). Like
1582, it is a black letter text.

Apart from correcting a few printing errors in the first
edition and making generally needless and minor changes
to the punctuation, spelling, and, here and there, the syntax,
1590 alters so as to make sensible the summary at the
beginning of the second chapter which in 1582 had referred,
inexplicably, to Chapter Six, and cuts two very significant
passages, ll. 628–70 ('that all . . . threatening') and ll. 683–
702 ('It is . . . blessed'). These cuts neatly eliminate all
the 'undecent words', as Munday terms them, spoken by
one of the priests at the College in his attack upon Elizabeth
and some of her chief ministers, which Munday had reported
at almost 'undecent' length in 1582. They were effected
after the relevant area of the text had been set up in its
original form, and necessitated the cancellation of Sheet C.
1590 replaces the first of these cuts with 'to be set down
according as he rehearsed them, would move offence'.
Necessarily, the paragraph 'It is not . . . blessed', which
refers to the offending passage, must also be left out.

Both passages initially would have appeared on the first
three or four pages of Sheet C. This sheet now has to be
reset to disguise the cutting of a substantial amount of
material that in 1582 occupied a total of fifty-one lines.
Accordingly, C1–C3ᵛ are set up with a measure of type
8 mm narrower than in the rest of 1590 and occupying on
C1–C3 thirty-five instead of the standard thirty-seven or
thirty-eight lines (the number varies between and within

formes). Chapter Two now ends halfway down C3ᵛ and Chapter Three begins on C4, which is set up with a normal measure of type and thirty-seven lines, presumably following line-for-line C4 in the cancelled sheet. Since half of C3ᵛ is still blank, a printer's ornament is inserted (space permitting, the normal procedure in 1590 is not to begin a new chapter on a new page).

It is interesting to speculate on the reasons behind the cancellation of Sheet C. There is some evidence to suggest that Charlewood was not acting on the authority of Munday, who may well have had nothing to do with the second edition of his book. With the possible exception of the revised summary at the head of Chapter Two, none of the readings peculiar to 1590 shows any indication of Munday's authority. Had he been consulted about the second edition it is likely that he would have made changes of a different kind, involving the references to his companion on the journey to Rome, Thomas Nowell who, as I have shown, had by 1583 renounced the Catholic faith and, according to Catholic sources, become a spy against Catholics in England. Since Munday was acting at this time as a government spy and must have known of Nowell's return to the fold, it is unlikely that he would have left untouched his comments on Nowell's religious inclinations had he been consulted over the second edition.

It is much more likely that Charlewood acted on his own authority when he cancelled Sheet C, possibly after consultation with the publisher Ling. Whether or not he was a Catholic, he had certainly printed for Catholic authors, including Philip Howard, the Earl of Arundel. Celeste Turner Wright has pointed out that in 1583 he printed the former's *Defensative against the Poison of Supposed Prophesies*, and 'When this book caused the Catholic author to be imprisoned, on charges of treason and heresy, Charlewood can hardly have gone unscathed. Next year he left most of his presswork unsigned'.[19] It would not be remarkable if in 1590 he should have second thoughts about printing a second time material that, despite

[19] 'Young Anthony Mundy Again', p. 155.

Munday's having obtained 'the judgement of those of worship and learning on this behalf' (ll. 688–9), must have been highly offensive to the objects of its witticisms. Presumably it had been made clear to Charlewood at some stage that the crucial passage had already 'moved offence', as he puts it, in 1582. In view of the copy having already been 'seen and allowed' in June 1582, and in the absence of evidence that Munday or anyone else authorized the cuts, understandable caution on Charlewood's part would seem a plausible enough explanation for his decision to cancel the offending sheet.

The second edition introduces many more printing errors than it corrects. Few of its readings have been adopted in the present edition since, with the possible exception of the revised summary for the second chapter which I have incorporated, none shows any real evidence of authority.

The second edition was reprinted, without the marginal glosses and the woodcut illustrations (and without introduction or notes) in the first edition of the *Harleian Miscellany*, vii (1746), 128–58, and again in the second edition, vii (1811), 136–67.

Another reprint, this time of the 1582 edition, appeared in 1925 as one of the series of Bodley Head Quartos (London, 1922–6). It was edited, with a brief introduction but without notes, by G. B. Harrison and reproduced (Edinburgh, 1966) as part of the series Elizabethan and Jacobean Quartos.

In the present edition spelling has been conservatively modernized so as to affect pronunciation as little as possible. Thus, whereas 'intreaty' has become 'entreaty' and 'vild' has become 'vile', 'unpossible' and 'unreverent' are at a greater remove from their modern equivalents and have been retained, as has 'thorough' in the sense of 'through', since modernization would entail the loss of a syllable. 'Farder' has been changed to 'farther' where it occurs—a change that 1590 also makes. Munday employs 'Saint' and 'S.' arbitrarily throughout; I have regularized these to 'St.' throughout, except where the saint's name is in an Italian form distinct from the English form, when I use 'S.'—thus

'S. Maria Maggiore', 'S. Maria di Loreto'. I have modernized the punctuation to some extent and considerably lightened it. The colon, for example, is much used in the original edition and, while one can sometimes justify it where it suggests consequence or marks illustration, often it checks the flow of words to a marked degree, at least to the modern eye. Munday's use of the comma also seems excessive. Passages of direct speech are not contained within inverted commas in the first edition and although Munday's handling of them is usually unconfused, it is not always so. For this reason all direct speech is in inverted commas in this edition. I have substituted new paragraphing for the original where direct speech is involved and in a few other places where change seemed desirable, and I have italicized according to modern practice rather than Munday's. Most of the capital letters in the early editions have been reduced to lower case, and abbreviations such as tildes and ampersands have been silently expanded. A few minor typographical errors have been put right without comment—for example, omission of spacing between two words or insertion of a space within a word. Other typographical errors, including some noticed in the Errata in Harrison's reprint, were corrected at the press, and because the variants in the Huntington Library copy are all in their corrected state, that copy is the copy text for this edition. The side-notes have been included because they occasionally reveal information not in the sections of text they summarize or relate to—for example the side-notes at ll. 126 and 797. Notes to material within them are keyed to the line alongside which the side-note begins.

THE ENGLISH

Romayne Lyfe.

Diſcouering:

The liues of the Engliſhmen at
Roome: the orders of the English Semi-
minarie: *the diſſention betweene the Engliſh-*
men and the VVelshmen: the baniſhing of the Engliſhmen
out of Roome: *the Popes ſending for them againe:* a reporte of many of the paltrie Reliques in Roome:
their Vautes vnder the grounde: their holy
Pilgrimages: and a number other matters,
worthy to be read and regarded
of euery one.

(∴)

There vnto is added, *the cruell tiranny,* vſed
on an Engliſh man at Roome, his Chriſtian ſuffering and
notable Martirdome, for the Goſpell of Ieſus Chriſte,
in Anno. 1581. VVritten by A. M. ſometime
the Popes Scholler in the Seminarie among them.

Honos alit Artes.

Seene and allovved.

Imprinted at London, by *John Charle-*
weede, for Nicholas Ling : dwelling in Paules Church-
yarde, at the ſigne of the Maremaide.
Anno. 1582.

Title-page of the 1582 edition

THE ENGLISH

Romayne Lyfe.

Discouering:

The liues of the Englishmen at *Roome* :
the orders of the *English Seminarie* : the dissention betweene the Englishmen and the welch-
men : the banishing of the Englishemen out of *Rome* : the
Popes sending for them againe : a reporte of many of the
paltrie Reliques in Rome : theyr Vautes vnder the
ground: their holy Pilgrimages: and a number other matters, woorthie
to be read and regarded
of euery one.

(∴)

A: Woode: mert: cott:
oxon: 1646:

There vnto is added, the cruell tiranny, vsed
on an English man at *Rome*, his Christian suffering, and
notable Martirdome, for the Gospel of Iesus Christ,
in Anno 1581. VVritten by A.M. sometime
the Popes Scholler in the Seminarie among them.

Honos alit Artes,

Seene and allowed.

Imprinted at London, by *John Charl-*
woode for Nicholas Ling : dwelling in
Paules Church-yarde.
Anno. 1590.   712.

Title-page of the 1590 edition

To the Right Honourable Sir Thomas Brom-
ley, Knight, Lord Chancellor of England;
William, Lord Burghley and Lord Treasurer;
Robert, Earl of Leicester, with all the rest of
Her Majesty's Most Honourable Privy Council, 5
  A. M. wisheth a happy race in continual
      honour, and the fulness of God's
         blessing in the Day of Joy.

This book, Right Honourable, as I have been
careful to note down nothing in it that might 10
impeach me either with error or untruth,
malice or affection to any, but even have
ordered the same according to certainty and
knowledge; so when I had fully finished it,
and done the uttermost of my endeavour 15
therein, I considered with myself, I was to
present the same to such personages of honour,
wisdom, and gravity as, did malice rule me,
they could quickly espy it, or affecting myself
to any, they would soon discern it; then would 20
honour reprove me for the one, and their
noble nature reprehend me in the other.
   To discharge myself of both these and pur-
chase the favour wherewith your Honours are
continually adorned, I directed my compass 25
by truth, persuading myself that albeit in

1-2. *Sir Thomas Bromley*] 1530-87, Lord Chancellor
1579, entered House of Lords 1582, and later presided over
the trial of Mary, Queen of Scots, 1586.
   3. *William, Lord Burghley*] William Cecil, 1520-98,
Elizabeth's chief minister, Baron of Burghley from 1571 and
Lord High Treasurer from 1572.
   4. *Robert, Earl of Leicester*] Robert Dudley, 1532?-88.
Elizabeth's favourite, created Baron Denbigh and Earl of
Leicester, 1564.
   6. *race*] course of life.
   11. *impeach*] discredit.
   25-6. *directed . . . by*] steered to the course of.

some, *veritas odium parit*, yet in your Honours, *magna est veritas et prevalet.*

30 Few words sufficeth your wisdoms, and circumstance without substance may incur disliking: according as when I presented your Honours with my book called the *Discovery of Campion*, I promised, so now in my *English Roman Life*, I have performed, thinking 35 myself in as safe security under your honourable favour as Ulysses supposed himself under the buckler of Ajax.

Your Honours' ever in duty,

Anthony Munday

27. veritas odium parit] truth creates animosity.

28. magna . . . prevalet] great is truth and it prevails. 3 Esdras 4:41 in the Vulgate (where 3 and 4 Esdras form an appendix).

30. *circumstance*] circumlocution.

31-3. *as . . . promised*] in *Discovery* Munday had mentioned the imminent appearance of 'a book, which by the grace of God shall come forth shortly, entitled, *The English Roman Life*' in which the activities of English Catholics abroad 'shall be truly and not maliciously reported' (C4^{r}).

36-7. *as . . . Ajax*] in the *Iliad*, xi. 482-6, Ajax shields the wounded Odysseus (Ulysses) against the Trojans. The shield of Ajax was of huge dimensions.

The thing long promised, gentle reader, is now
performed at last, and that which my adversaries thought I would never set forth, to their
disproof and thy profit, I have now published.
Thou shalt find a number of matters compre- 45
hended within this small volume: some, that
will irritate the mind of any good subject, and
therefore to be read with regard; others,
importing the whole course of our Englishmen's lives in Rome, with the odd conceits 50
and crafty jugglings of the Pope (whereto our
Englishmen are likewise conformable), they
are in such true and certain order set down, as
if thou were there thyself to behold them. I
will not use many words; now thou hast it, read 55
advisedly, condemn not rashly, and if thou
thinkest me worthy any thanks for my pains,
then friendly bestow it on me.

Thine in courtesy,
Anthony Munday   60

45-6. *comprehended*] contained.
47. *irritate*] provoke to action.
49. *course*] practice.
50-1. *odd . . . jugglings*] strange conceptions and artful
deceptions.
52. *conformable*] in conformity.
56. *advisedly*] judiciously, with full and calm consider-
ation.
58. *friendly*] adv., like a friend.

THE ENGLISH ROMAN LIFE,

discoursing the lives of such Englishmen as by
secret escape leave their own country to live
in Rome under the servile yoke of the Pope's
government. Also after what manner they 65
spend their time there, practising and
daily looking for the overthrow
and ruin of their Princess
and country.

☛ First, how the author left his native country 70
of England, betaking himself to travel, and
what happened in his journey toward Rome.

CHAPTER 1

Because a number have been desirous to
understand the success of my journey to 75
Rome, and a number beside are doubtful
whether I have been there or no, albeit the
proofs thereof sufficiently are extant to be
seen: as well to content the one as remove the
doubt of the other, I will (God aiding me) here 80
set down such a certainty thereof that if it
happen not to please both, yet, if they will, it
may profit both.

Whenas desire to see strange countries, as also
affection to learn the languages, had persuaded 85
me to leave my native country, and not any
other intent or cause, God is my record: I
committed the small wealth I had into my
purse, a traveller's weed on my back, the whole

62. *discoursing*] treating. 1590 has *Discovering*.
66. *practising*] plotting.
75. *success*] outcome.
89. *weed*] garment.

90 state and condition of my journey to God's appointment and, being accompanied with one Thomas Nowell, crossed the seas from England to Boulogne in France. From thence we travelled to Amiens, in no small danger, 95 standing to the mercy of despoiling soldiers who went robbing and killing thorough the country, the camp being by occasion broken up at that time. Little they left us, and less would have done, by the value of our lives, 100 had not a better booty come than we were at that time: the soldiers preparing towards them, whom they saw better provided for their necessity, offered us the leisure to escape which we refused not, being left bare enough 105 both of coin and clothes. But as then we stood not to account on our loss, it sufficed us that we had our lives, whereof being not a little glad, we set the better leg before lest they should come back again and rob us of 110 them too.

The camp broken up, the soldiers met with us and robbed us, and hardly did we escape with our lives.

90. *state and condition*] nature and circumstances.

91. *appointment*] direction.

92. *Thomas Nowell*] The *Liber Ruber,* the list of students in the English College, Rome, in which Nowell appears as item 51, mentions that he came from the diocese of Lichfield, and was eighteen years old on 29 Apr. 1579. Laurence Nowell, Dean of Lichfield (and brother of Alexander Nowell, the Dean of St. Paul's) had a son of this name, but he was baptized on 5 Apr. 1573. See Ralph Churton, *Life of Alexander Nowell* (Oxford, 1809), p. 233. Robert Persons's *Memoirs (C.R.S. Miscellanea,* iv [1907], 82-5) and the *Liber Ruber* entry reveal that Nowell was dismissed in April 1583 as unsuitable for the English College and later became a spy against Catholics in England.

93. s.n. *hardly*] barely.

95. *standing to*] submitting ourselves to.

95. *soldiers*] Sporadic local fighting, especially between Catholics and Huguenots, was common in many parts of France at this period. (See R. B. Wernham, ed., *The New Cambridge Modern History*, iii [Cambridge, 1968], 293).

105-6. *as . . . loss*] as we were in no position to think much of our loss.

108. *set . . . before*] a version of the proverb 'to put one's best foot foremost'; make all haste. Tilley, F570.

This our misfortune urged us to remembrance of our former quiet being in England, carefully tended by our parents and lovingly esteemed among our friends, all which we undutifully regarding, rewarded us with the 115 rod of our own negligence; being as then fearful of all company on the way, such cruel and heavy spectacles was still before our eyes, but yet this did somewhat comfort us, we had nothing worth the taking from us but our 120 lives, which we had good hope to save, either by their pity or our own humble persuasion.

Many men robbed and slain by the soldiers, which made us travel in no small fear.

When we were come to Amiens, we were given to understand that there was an old English priest in the town, whose name was 125 Master Woodward, of whom we persuaded ourselves, for country's sake, to find some courtesy; in hope whereof we enquired for his lodging and at last found him. After such

The priest of whom I have made mention in my Discovery of Campion.

salutations as pass between countrymen at 130 their meeting, I began to tell him how we had left our country for the earnest desire we had to see foreign dominions, how we had been spoiled by the way of all that we had, and that we hoped for some friendship at his 135 hands, which if God vouchsafed us safe return should not be cast out of remembrance.

'Alas my friends', quoth he, 'I am your countryman I will not deny, but not such a one as you take me for. I am a poor priest, 140

117–18. *cruel... spectacles*] distressing and gloomy sights, specifically, perhaps, the 'Many men robbed and slain' of 119 s.n.

127. *for country's sake*] i.e. as fellow Englishmen.

132–3. *the . . . dominions*] Munday is concerned lest the reader see a religious motive behind the journey. cf. above, ll. 84–7, 'Whenas desire to see strange countries, . . .'. This concern is understandably evident throughout *E.R.L.*

134. *spoiled*] robbed.

137. *should . . . remembrance*] It is tempting to read this as consciously ironic. As the side-note points out, Munday had already mentioned Woodward in *Discovery*.

and here I live for my conscience' sake, whereas, were things according as they should be, it
were better for me to be at home in mine own
country. And yet trust me, I pity to see any
145 of my countrymen lack, though I am not able
any way to relieve them: there be daily that
cometh this way to whom, according to my
ability, I am liberal, but they be such as you
are not, they come not for pleasure but for
150 profit, they come not to see every idle toy,
and to learn a little language, but to learn how
to save both their own and their friends' souls,
and such I would you were, then I could say
that to you, which (as you be) I may not.'
155 'Trust me, sir,' quoth I, 'I hope we have
learned to save our souls already, or else you
might esteem us in a very bad case.'
'If you have,' quoth he, 'it is the better for
you, but I fear me one day, they that teach
160 you to save your souls after that manner will
pay for it dearly, and you with them for
company.'
With these words, he began to wax somewhat melancholy, which I perceiving, and
165 remembering that our necessity stood not in
case to plead points of controversy, rather
sought to please him in hope of some liberality, than to contend with him (we being
unable) and so fall into farther danger. Where-
170 upon I desired him not to be offended at anything we had said, for we would gladly learn
anything that might benefit us, and beside,

146. *there be*] 'those' is understood.
150. *idle toy*] frivolous amusement.
159. *one day*] the Day of Judgement, with perhaps a
suggestion of an earthly retribution upon the Church of
England.
160. *that manner*] i.e. the Anglican manner.
165–6. *stood . . to*] left us in no position to.

would follow his counsel in any reasonable
cause. Then he began to be somewhat more
gently disposed, saying he could not greatly 175
blame us, if we were obstinate in our opinion,
coming from such a young hell as we did, but
he had good hope that ere long it would be
harrowed.

Then he willed us to walk with him and he 180
would bring us where we should lodge that
night, at his charges, all the way rehearsing
unto us how beneficial the Pope was to our
countrymen and how highly we might pleasure
ourselves, our friends and country, if we would 185
follow his counsel. Beside, such horrible and
unnatural speeches he used against Her
Majesty, her Honourable Council, and other
persons that he named, as the very remembrance maketh me blush, and my heart to 190
bleed. To all which we gave him the hearing,
but God knows, on my part, with what anguish
of mind: for I would have persuaded myself
that duty should have withheld the subject
from reviling his Princess, and nature from 195
slandering his own country; but it sufficeth,
where grace is absent, good qualities can never
be present. When we were come to our lodging, he talked with our hostess, what she
should provide for us, and afterward taking 200
his leave told us he would have more talk with
us in the morning; in the meantime, we should
think on that which he had opened to us, and

The priest used many circumstances of the Pope's liberality to our countrymen, as also what treasons was toward Her Majesty and the realm.

174. *cause*] concern; but 'course' (of action) seems
more appropriate here.
180. s.n. *used many circumstances*] cited many instances.
182. *charges*] expense.
186. *Beside*] In addition.
192. *on my part*] the first suggestion of what Munday
makes increasingly explicit: Nowell's Catholic tendencies.
193. *I . . . myself*] The construction seems awkward but
is paralleled by 'I would have thought'.
203. *opened*] revealed.

resolve ourselves on a certain determination, 205 for he meant us more good than we were beware of. He being departed, we fell to such simple cheer as was prepared for us, which was simple indeed, scant sufficient to the good stomachs we had to our victuals; but 210 because we had soon done, we went the sooner to bed, sparing as much time as we could in remembrance of the priest's words, till the weariness of our journey compelled us to take our rest.

A little sufficeth hunger where necessity is mistress of the feast.

215 In the morning the priest sent a poor fellow, whom he kept to make his bed and run about on his errands, to our lodging, that we should come unto his master presently, because he had occasion to go into the town, and his 220 return was uncertain, therefore he would speak with us before he went. Upon these so hasty summons we addressed ourselves towards him, finding him in his chamber reading upon his portas; to him we gave thanks for his courtesy, 225 promising to requite it if he came where we might do it. In brief, among great circumstance of talk, wherein he manifested the treason toward England, he behaved himself in speeches to us according as I have already 230 declared in my *Discovery of Campion*, where you may perceive the Pope's determination,

There you may read his words, at large set down.

---

204. *resolve ... determination*] come to a definite decision.

206. *beware*] aware.

207. *simple cheer*] humble food. Munday then plays on the word 'simple', using it in its sense of insignificant or slight.

209. *good ... victuals*] good appetite we had for food.

211-14. *sparing ... rest*] Munday at his sarcastic best.

218. *presently*] immediately.

220. *uncertain*] indefinite in point of time.

222. *addressed ourselves*] went directly.

224. *portas*] breviary, from which Woodward, being a priest, is bound each day to recite the Divine Office.

226-7. *great ... talk*] much detailed discussion.

227. *manifested*] plainly revealed.

and our Englishmen's unnatural consent, to
be traitors to their own Princess, to shorten
her life, and overthrow their native country
where they were born.   235

When he had mightily besieged us with a
multitude, as well threatenings as persuasions,
to conform ourselves under that obedience, as
well to avoid peril that might otherwise happen
as also to gain somewhat toward our relief, we 240
promised him to do as he would have us, and
to go whither he would appoint us. Whereupon he presently wrote two letters to Doctor
Allen at Reims: one of them concerned our
preferment there, how we should be enter-   245
tained into the English seminary and take the
orders of priesthood, because we might do
good in our country another day. The other
letter was of such news as he heard out of
England, how matters went forward to their   250
purpose, and beside, other things which I am
not to speak of here, because they are not to
be read of everyone.

233-4. *to shorten her life*] From 1581 there were certainly several carefully laid plots against Elizabeth's life,
but it is doubtful whether there were any as early as 1578-9.
It is nevertheless logical that some Catholic exiles in their less
generous moments should give voice to the hope that Elizabeth might be removed by one means or another.

238. *conform . . . obedience*] comply with the authority
or Rome.

239. *peril . . . happen*] perhaps then and there, or later in
the journey.

240. *relief*] i.e. of the distress that the theft of their
belongings had placed them in.

243-4. *Doctor Allen at Reims*] Cardinal William Allen,
1532-94, the most eminent of the Catholic exiles. He opened
the seminary at Douai in 1568, where he taught as Doctor
and Professor of Divinity and oversaw the production of
what was to become the Douai-Reims Bible. In 1578, shortly
before the time Munday is writing about here, the seminary
was forced by the antagonism of Calvinists to move to Reims.
Allen was instrumental in the development of the English
College in Rome, which became his home in 1585.

245. *preferment*] advancement.

245-6. *entertained*] admitted.

These letters finished, and sealed up with
255 singing cake, he delivered unto us, saying 'I
thank God that I am ordained the man both
to save your souls and a number of your
friends there in England, whom I could wish
here present with you, for that I pity their
260 estate, as well that they are in, as that which
is worse, and I fear me will fall on them
shortly.'

I put up the letters, and gave him to understand that we could hardly travel from thence
265 to Reims, having nothing wherewithal we
might bear our charges. 'Trust me,' quoth he,
'and I have done as much for you as I am able,
for I have nothing here but to serve mine own
necessity.' Then we offered to sell our cloaks,
270 which the soldiers against their wills had left
us. 'Indeed,' quoth he, 'to travel in your cloaks
will do nothing but hinder you; I will send my
man to a friend of mine' (as much to say, as
his chest) 'to see what money he can get for
275 them.'

The fellow took our cloaks, after his
master had whispered him in the ear, and
went down the stairs, returning quickly with
two French crowns which the priest delivered

254-5. *sealed* . . *cake*] 'singing cake' and 'singing bread'
were terms for the wafer used in the mass, apparently because
it was made during chanting. See *Brewer's Dictionary of
Phrase and Fable* (rev. edn., London, 1970), p. 1004. The
O.E.D. gives a secondary use, 'as a wafer for sealing with.
Obs.', quoting the phrase in *E.R.L.* as its only example.

258. there *ed*: here *1, 2*.

260. *estate*] condition.

260-1. *that which is worse*] These words as Munday
reports them are deliberately ambiguous, constituting one of
his many 'proofs' of a fearsome retribution being planned
against England.

263. *put up*] pocketed.

274. *chest*] coffer.

279. *two French crowns*] the 'French crown', properly
écu, fluctuated in value but was roughly equivalent to the
English crown.

to us with four or five French sous out of his 280
own purse; so, willing us to do his commendations to Doctor Allen, and to labour earnestly
in that we went about, Master Woodward and
we parted, he into the town, and we on our
journey.   285
   When we were about three or four miles
from Amiens we sat down on the side of a hill,
recounting what the priest had said to us, as
also the cause why he sent us to Reims; the
remembrance of the true and undoubted 290
religion used in our own country, and wherein
we were trained up, was of force sufficient to
persuade us from yielding to that which we
judged rather to be a mummery, and derision
of the true doctrine, than otherwise: so that 295
(notwithstanding many matters my companion
alleged unto me, what danger we might come
unto, if we went not to deliver the letters, as
also the hard penury we should find in travel,
being destitute of money, apparel, and all 300
other needful things) by the only appointment
of God, who no doubt put it in my mind at
that time, I willed him to follow me, and come
woe, want, misery, or any other calamity, I
would never leave him to the death. But if 305
any exercise might get it, any pains compass it,
or the extreme shift of begging attain it, I
would do all myself whereby to maintain us,
only that he would but bear me company, for
I would try all means that might be ere I would 310
forsake my faith.
   This to be true I am sure and certain himself
will not deny, who, seeing my earnest entreaty

Marginalia:

Great liberality. *(at line 280–281)*

This to be true, albeit he now be my utter enemy, I am sure he will not deny. *(at lines 301–305)*

---

280. *sous* ed: souses *1, 2.* Their value, or lack of it, is
proverbial.
   281–2. *do his commendations*] give his regards.
   294. *mummery*] 'Often applied to religious ritual regarded
as silly or hypocritical.' *O.E.D.* Mummery, 2.
   297. *alleged unto me*] cited for me, drew my attention to.
   301. *only appointment*] special direction.

and the promises I made to the uttermost of
315 my power, agreed to go with me, and so we
left the way to Reims and went on straight to
Paris.

In Paris we met with a Frenchman who
could speak a little broken English and he
320 conducted us where my Lord the English
Ambassador lay, to whom I gave the letters,
and after certain talk he used with us, he
bestowed his honourable liberality upon us,
wishing us to return back again into England.
325 Leaving my Lord and walking into the city,
we met certain English gentlemen; some of
them for the knowledge they had of me in
England showed themselves very courteous to
me, both in money, lodging and other neces-
330 saries. And through them we became acquainted with a number of Englishmen more who
lay in the city, some in colleges, and some at
their own houses, where, using daily company
among them sometime at dinner, and some-
335 time at supper, we heard many girds and nips
against our country of England, Her Majesty
very unreverently handled in words and certain
of her Honourable Council undutifully
termed.
340 Great talk they had about Doctor Saunders,
who they said, either as then was, or shortly

It is a good help, to
meet a friend in a
strange country
when a man is in
some need.

320-1. *the English Ambassador*] Sir Amias Paulet, 1536?–
88, ambassador to France, 1576-9.

322. *used*] engaged in.

332. *colleges*] communities or corporations 'of clergy
living together on a foundation for religious service'. *O.E.D.*
College, 3. But Munday may simply mean that these Englishmen lived in some communal fashion.

335. *girds and nips*] sarcastic comments. The two words
are practically synonymous here.

340-52. *Doctor Saunders . . . might be*] Nicholas Sanders,
or Saunders, 1530?–81, was among other things a historian
and Regius Professor of Theology at Louvain. His direct
activities against Elizabeth date from 1573 when he was
working in Madrid for her replacement by a Catholic. Six

would be, arrived in Ireland, how he had an
army of Spaniards with him, and how himself
under the Pope's standard would give such an
attempt there, as soon after should make all 345
England to quake; beside, there were certain
Englishmen gone to the Pope for more aid, if
need should be, at whose return certain noblemen, Englishmen then being in those parts,
whose names I omit for divers causes, would 350
prosecute the matter with as much speed as
might be.

The very same did the priest at Amiens give
us to understand of, almost in every point
agreeing with this, which made us to doubt, 355
because in every man's mouth Her Majesty
still was aimed at in such manner as I tremble
and shake to think on their words. All this
time that we remained amongst them, divers
of the gentlemen and others (who were like 360
factors for the Pope, as Master Woodward at
Amiens, Doctor Bristow at Douai, and Doctor
Allen at Reims were, to increase his seminaries
with as many Englishmen as they might) very
earnestly persuaded us to travel to Rome, 365
assuring us that we should be there entertained
to our high contentment; beside, they would

Any subject that hath either fear of God or love to his prince would quake to hear their traitorous devices.

The Devil wanteth no instruments to help his cause.

years later he was in Ireland, promoting rebellion there and
gaining the support of Gerald Fitzgerald, Earl of Desmond.
Sanders landed in Kerry in 1579 not with 'an army of Spaniards' but with James Fitzgerald (Fitzmaurice), d. 1579, and
a band of followers, his banner ('the Pope's standard')
blessed by Gregory XIII. A respectable force of Spaniards
and Italians sent by the Curia did arrive in Kerry in 1580,
but these quickly surrendered and were put to the sword.
Sanders died, his mission a failure, in 1581.

355. *doubt*] be fearfully apprehensive.

357. *still*] constantly.

360-1. *like factors*] similar agents.

362. *Doctor Bristow*] Richard Bristow, 1538-81, took
his D.D. at Douai in 1575, having earlier been appointed
by Allen as moderator of studies in the seminary. But by this
time Bristow must have moved to Reims along with Allen,
for when Allen moved the seminary there he placed it under
Bristow's care.

give us letters for our better welcome thither.

370 We were soon entreated to take the journey on us because we thought if we could go to Rome and return safely again into England we should accomplish a great matter, the place being so far off and the voyage so dangerous.

375 Upon our agreement to undertake the travel, we received of everyone liberally toward the bearing of our charges, and letters we had to Master Doctor Lewis in Rome, the Archdeacon of Cambrai, and to Doctor Morris, then the rector of the English Hospital or College in

380 Rome, that we might there be preferred among the English students.

Taking our leave of them, and yielding them thanks for their great courtesy, we journeyed to Lyons, where in the house of one

385 Master Deacon the words were spoken by Henry Orton, one of them condemned, and yet living in the Tower, which in my other

By their persuasions and liberality they win a number daily to them.

377-80. *Doctor Lewis . . . College in Rome*] Owen Lewis (or Lewis Owen), 1532-94, who at this time resided in Rome, had been Regius Professor of Law at Douai and later canon of the cathedral at Cambrai and Archdeacon of Hainault. He subsequently became a vicar-general in the diocese of Cardinal Carlo Borromeo, Archbishop of Milan (below, l. 389). 'Doctor Morris', commonly so called, was Maurice Clenocke (or Clynog), d. 1580?, born in Wales and educated at Oxford. He became warden of the Hospital of the English Pilgrims—the English College—at Rome, which Gregory XIII converted into a seminary in 1577-8, making Clenocke, on Lewis's recommendation, its first rector. The English students accused Clenocke of favouring the minority of Welsh students, and as a result of the open mutiny (February–March, 1579) in which Munday played a principal role and which he describes in Chapter Six, the English College was placed under the government of the Jesuits and Clenocke replaced by Alfonso Agazzari (appointed 23 Apr. 1579). Clenocke went to Rouen *c.* 1580 and was drowned *en route* to Spain.

385. *Master Deacon*] unidentified.

386. *Henry Orton*] Although originally sentenced to death, along with Edmund Campion and others, Orton was ultimately banished on 15 Jan. 1585 (*C.S.P. Dom. 1591-4*, p. 223). According to *Discovery* he referred to Elizabeth as a usurper, adding that 'even so should she ere long be used' (DI^r).

book I have avouched. From thence we went
to Milan, where in the Cardinal Borromeo's
Palace we found the lodging of a Welshman 390
named Doctor Robert Griffin, a man there
had in a good account, and confessor to the
aforesaid cardinal. By him we were very
courteously entertained and sent to the house
of an English priest in the city, named Master 395
Harris, who likewise bestowed on us very
gentle acceptance, as also three English gentlemen, who lay in his house, being very lately
returned from Rome; they likewise both in
cost and courtesy behaved themselves like 400
gentlemen unto us during the time that we
made our abode in Milan.

> There are English-
> men almost in every
> city by the way.

Our coming to Milan was on Christmas
even, and having lain that night at an *osteria*
where Master Harris appointed us, on Christ- 405
mas day we dined with Doctor Griffin, where
we had great cheer, and like welcome. In the
dinner-time he moved many questions unto
us, as concerning the estate of England, if we
heard of any wars towards and how the 410
Catholics thrived in England; and at the last,
quoth he, 'Have you not seen three gentlemen
that lie at Master Harris his house?'

> The talk that Doctor
> Griffin had with us,
> being at dinner with
> him.

'Yes that we have,' quoth I, 'to us they

389–90. *Cardinal Borromeo's Palace*] St. Carlo Borromeo,
1534–84, Archbishop of Milan, played a prominent part in
the final sessions of the Council of Trent.
391. *Doctor Robert Griffin*] properly, according to the
Dictionary of Welsh Biography (Oxford, 1959), pp. 857–8,
Gruffydd Robert, 1522?–1610? After Elizabeth's accession
he left for the Continent with Maurice Clenocke, spent some
time as a chaplain in the English Hospital at Rome, and later
became a divinity canon in Milan Cathedral and a confessor
to Cardinal Borromeo.
395–6. *Master Harris*] unidentified.
397. *gentle acceptance*] kind reception.
404. lain *ed*: lien *1, 2*.
404. osteria] inn, specifically in Italy. Munday is beginning
to use Italian words.
410. *towards*] imminent.

415 seem marvellous courteous, and offer us such
friendship as we have never deserved.'

'Oh,' quoth he, 'if all things had fallen right
to their expectation, they would have been
jolly fellows. I am sure you have heard what
420 credit Captain Stukely was in with the Pope,
and how he was appointed with his army, to
invade England; he being slain in the battle of
the King of Portugal, things went not forward
according as they should have done. These
425 three gentlemen came forth of the north parts
of England, taking upon them to go forward
with that which Stukely had enterprised,
which was, to have the Pope's army committed
to their conduction, and so they would overrun
430 England at their pleasure; then they would
make kings and dukes and earls, everyone that
they thought well of. To help them forward
in this matter, they purchased the letters of
Doctor Saunders, Doctor Allen, Doctor Bris-
435 tow, and others who thought very well of their
intent and therefore furthered them in their
letters so much as they might, to Doctor
Lewis, Doctor Morris, Doctor Morton, and

An unnatural desire
of men to seek the
ruin of their own
country.

The secret seducing
priests win a number
to join in their
traitorous intent.

420. Stukely 2: Sukely 1.
420-4. *Stukely . . . done*] Thomas Stukely, 1525?-78,
was one of the most extraordinary adventurers of the time.
After successfully negotiating with the Pope on the means for
an invasion of Ireland, he embarked on 4 Mar. 1578 from Civita
Vecchia with a galleon and about 600 men. Having struggled
into Lisbon Stukely failed to get the young Portuguese king,
Sebastian, to give him more seaworthy ships. Instead, the
king persuaded him to join him in his Moroccan campaign,
in which both men died at the Battle of Alcazar, 4 Aug. 1578.
Stukeley's exploits were used in *The Famous History of the
Life and Death of Captain Thomas Stukely* (1605) which
may have been the play performed by the Admiral's Men
during 1596 and 1597. (Ed. Judith C. Levinson [Oxford,
1974], p. viii. Malone Society Reprints.)
433. *purchased*] procured.
438. *Doctor Morton*] Nicholas Morton, *fl.* 1586; left
England in 1558 on Elizabeth's accession, returning in 1569
to help promote the Northern rebellion. Subsequently
resident at Rome.

divers other doctors and gentlemen at Rome, all of them very earnestly following the suit 440 hereof to the Pope's Holiness, informing him how they had already won such a number in England to join with them when the matter came to pass, that granting them His Holiness' army, they would presently overrun all 445 England and yield it wholly into his hand. But when the Pope had scanned on this hasty business, well noting the simple and arrogant behaviour of the men, and their unlikelihood of performing these things, even according as 450 they deserved, they were denied their request and sent away without any recompense. The Pope was not to trust to any such as they; he well knows England is too strong yet, and till the people be secretly persuaded, as I doubt 455 not but there is a good number, and more and more still shall be, by the priests are sent over daily, and they must war within, while others hold them play without: till then England will not be conquered any way.' 460

The Pope seeketh to accomplish his desire by the subject that must betray his own country.

Other talk we had, not here to be rehearsed, but truly it would astonish a heart of adamant, to hear the horrible treasons invented against Her Majesty and this realm, and so greedily followed by our own countrymen. But some 465 perhaps will demand how we behaved ourselves to come to the knowledge of such traitorous intentions, judging that they would rather keep them secret than reveal them to any: to answer such as so do question, thus it 470 was.

When I was at Paris, the gentlemen took me to be a gentleman's son here in England,

The mean whereby they made me acquainted with all their devices.

447. *scanned on*] formed an opinion of.
448. *simple and arrogant*] foolish and presumptuous.
458–9. others hold 2: other holds 1.
459. *hold . . . without*] keep them occupied outside.
461. *rehearsed*] related.

whom I refuse here to name, but as it seemed,
475 they were somewhat persuaded of him. I
perceiving they took me for his son, called
myself by his name, where through I was the
better esteemed, and beside, loved as I had
been he indeed. When they understood my
480 fellow's name to be Thomas Nowell, they
whispered among themselves, and said un-
doubtedly he was kin to Master Nowell the
Dean of Paul's; and if they wist certainly that
he were so they would use him in such gentle
485 order as they would keep him there, so that
one day he should stand and preach against
his kinsman. This suppose, serving so well our
necessity, we were glad to use, which made us
well thought on of all, and keeping company
490 so familiarly with them we were made acquainted with a number more matters than
may here be expressed.

The treason against England was common in every Englishman's mouth.

While we were in Milan we visited Master
Doctor Parker, who likewise told us the same

475. *persuaded*] assured.

477. *his name*] Munday continues to use this name in
Rome. Its Latinized form, as we now know from the papers
of Cardinal Morone, where names are regularly Latinized, was
Antonius Auleus. See Anthony Kenny, 'Antony Munday in
Rome', *Recusant History*, vi (1962), 159. Given the probable
contemporary English pronunciation of Latin *au*, it seems
likely to me that Munday called himself Hawley. According
to his *Memoirs*, *C.R.S. Miscellanea*, ii (1906), Robert Persons
spent Christmas 1573 in London with 'a distinguished man
called Hawley' (p. 21), whose son James was with Persons at
Oxford and who was 'living to this day [1601] in good worship' (p. 47). In 1594 a Mrs. Hawley was among some Catholics smuggled across the Channel. See *C.S.P.Dom. 1591-4*,
p. 409. Either may have had connections in Staffordshire, the
home of Munday's pretended family (below, ll. 740-6).

482. *Master Nowell*] Alexander Nowell, 1507?-1602,
Dean of St. Paul's from 1560.

483. *wist certainly*] knew for sure.

484-5. *gentle order*] generous fashion.

487. *suppose*] supposition.

494. *Doctor Parker*] Thomas Parker, *fl.* 1581. The *D.N.B.*
mentions that he was living in Milan in 1581, but this reference establishes his residence there in 1578.

tale that Doctor Griffin had before rehearsed; 495
beside, he told us that priests were appointed
from Rome and Reims for England and that
ere long they should be sent.

Soon after we departed thence, to Bologna,
Florence, Siena, and so to Rome, where how 500
we were received the chapter following shall
amply unfold. Thus, as well to certify the
incredulous, as also to content those desirous
how I attained to Rome, I have briefly done
my good will to please both.   505

You have heard herein how at sundry places
and by several speeches there was a general
agreement of treason, expected and daily
looked for, to the harm of our gracious sov-
ereign and hurt of her whole realm. All these 510
matters we heard before we came to Rome,
from whence the treason should chiefly
proceed; we seeing such devilish devices to
be talked on by the way, we might well judge
Rome to be Hell itself, in that all things should 515
go forward as it was there determined. You
are not altogether ignorant of their intents at
Rome, for that my other book hath truly
revealed some of their traitorous and disloyal
practices, and such as modesty will suffer me 520
to utter, and you to read, you shall here find
faithfully discoursed.

502. *certify*] assure.
518. *my other book*] *Discovery.*
522. *discoursed*] treated, set forth at length.

(✒ The author, being come to Rome, entreth into conference with a priest in the English
525 College who showeth him a paper, containing villainous and traitorous determinations against Her Majesty's most royal person, her Honourable Council, and other persons of credit and account.

530   CHAPTER 2

Our entrance into Rome was upon Candlemas even, whenas it drew somewhat towards night, for which cause we refused as then to go to the English College, taking up our lodging in
535 an *osteria* somewhat within the city and deter-
mining to visit the English house on the next morning. On the morrow by enquiring, we found the English College, where after we were once entered we had a number about us
540 quickly, to know what news in England, and how all matters went there. Not long had we stood talking with them, but one entered the College, with a great many of wax candles in

A present of holy
candles   brought
from the Pope to
the English students.

523-9. *entreth ... account*] 2. Most of the corresponding summary in 1 refers, inexplicably, to Chapter Six. It reads: 'The author being come to Rome, after what manner he was received into the English Seminary. The emulation and dissention between the Welshmen and the Englishmen in the College, their banishment out of Rome, and the Pope's sending for them again, as you shall read hereafter.'

531-2. *Candlemas even*] 1 Feb. 1579.

534. *the English College*] on the Via Monserrato. It was founded in 1362 as a hospice for English pilgrims and continued to offer this service after conversion, by Gregory XIII in 1577-8, into a seminary for training English priests. In 1579 it was placed under Jesuit control in circumstances described by Munday in Chapter Six, although it did not formally become a college until 1580. At the time of Munday's arrival there were forty students there.

543. *wax candles*] The feast of Candlemas commemorates

his hand, who gave them to understand that
the Pope had sent to every scholar in the 545
College a candle which that day at high mass
he had hallowed, for it was Candlemas day.
They receiving them with great account, both
of the Pope's favour, as also the holiness they
credited to consist in the candles, went every 550
one to lay them up in their chambers; in the
meantime Master Doctor Morris the rector of
the house came to us, to whom we delivered
the letter sent to him on our behalf from Paris,
which when he had read, he said we were wel- 555
come, allowing us the eight days' entertainment in the Hospital, which by the Pope was
granted to such Englishmen as came thither.
Then he brought us to Doctor Lewis, the
Archdeacon of Cambrai, to whom we delivered 560
his letter likewise, and with him we stayed
dinner, ignorant whether he were an Englishman or no, for that he gave us our entertainment in Latin, demanded a number of
questions of us in Latin, and beside, dined 565
with us in Latin; whereat we marvelled, till
after dinner, he had us walk to the College
again with Doctor Morris, in English.
We were no sooner come to the College
but the scholars, who had already dined, and 570
were walking together in the court, came

the purification of the Blessed Virgin and the presentation of
Christ in the Temple forty days after his birth. Beeswax
candles are blessed as the day's distinctive rite. See the *Oxford
Dictionary of the Christian Church* (Oxford, 1971), p. 226,
Candlemas.

552. *Master Doctor Morris*] Maurice Clenocke. See note
to ll. 377–80 above.

556–8. *eight days'... thither*] Despite the rector Maurice
Clenocke's objections, Munday and Nowell managed to stay
on after the eight days, apparently as 'humanistae' or grammar
students, although their exact status is not clear. See Kenny,
'Antony Munday in Rome', p. 158, where relevant documen-
tation is presented; and Giuseppe Galigani, 'La *English
Romayne Lyfe* di A. Mundy', *Rivista di letterature moderne
e comparate* (Florence), xviii (1965), 114 ff.

about us, every one demanding so many
questions that we knew not which to answer
first; at last one of them took my fellow aside,
575 and one of the priests likewise desired to talk
with me, because he said he knew my father
well enough, using the name that I did; so, he
and I sitting together in the garden, among
other talk he asked of me, wherefore I came
580 to Rome?

'Trust me sir,' quoth I, 'only for the desire
I had to see it, that when I came home again,
I might say, once in my life I have been at
Rome.'

585 'Then I perceive', quoth he, 'you come
more upon pleasure than any devotion, more
desirous to see the city than to learn the
virtues contained in it; in sooth I see, you
remain in the same wildness you did when I
590 lay at your father's house, but I do not doubt
now we have you here to make you a staid
man ere you depart, that your father may
have joy of you and all your friends receive
comfort by you.'

595 'Indeed sir,' quoth I, 'I have always addicted
my mind to so many youthful devices, that I
little regarded any religion, which my parents
seeing, and fearing I would never be bridled,
sent me over to Paris, where I should remain
600 at my book. But there I found gentlemen of
mine acquaintance who wished me to travel
hither, whereto I quickly gave my consent,
being, as I have told you, desirous to see a
thing so famous.'

605 'I think very well', quoth he, 'of your words,
as well for your parents' sake as also your
own. But this I will say unto you, there ought
none to come hither, the place being so holy,
ancient, and famous, but only such as with
610 earnest endeavour seek and thirst after the
Catholic faith: being here taught and main-

The talk one of the
priests had with me
in the garden.

Mine   own   tale,
which so well as I
could, I made to
agree   with   the
priest's discourse.

tained, according as Christ ordained it, the
apostles delivered it, Peter himself planted it,
and all the fathers of the Church since have
followed it. They must denounce that damn- 615
able heresy, crept into the Church of England,
that proud usurping Jezebel', meaning our
dread and gracious Princess, 'whom', quoth he,
'God reserveth to make her a notable spectacle
to the whole world, for keeping that good 620
Queen of Scots from her lawful rule; but I
hope ere long the dogs shall tear her flesh,
and those that be her props and upholders.'

*Here may you be-
hold what unrever-
ent speeches they
can afford Her
Majesty.*

Then drawing a paper out of his pocket, he
said, 'I have a bead-roll of them here, who little 625
knows what is providing for them, and I hope
shall not know, till it fall upon them.' Then
he read their names unto me, which, that all
may perceive the villainous and traitorous
minds of our own countrymen, so many of 630
them as I can call to memory I will set down,
even in the same manner as he read them. But
first I must crave pardon of those honourable personages to whom the words do offer
great abuse, and whom I unfeignedly rever- 635
ence and honour: that they would not admit
any evil conceit against me, but in the noble
nature wherewith they are daily adorned, I,
being but the reporter, may be pardoned and
not reproved.   640

*A paper of the names
of such noblemen of
Her Majesty's Coun-
cil whom they meant
to persecute when
their intent came to
pass in England.*

617-22. *Jezebel . . . flesh*] The biblical Jezebel's body
was devoured by dogs (2 Kgs 9:30-7), fulfilling the prophecy
of 1 Kgs 21:23.
  620-1. *keeping . . . rule*] Elizabeth kept Mary prisoner
because Mary posed a real threat to the English throne, but
the priest is probably referring to Mary's 'lawful rule' of
Scotland, which she was forced to abdicate in 1567 in favour
of her son, James VI.
  625. *bead-roll*] list (originally a list of persons to be prayed
for, and therefore used here ironically).
  637. *evil conceit*] ill opinion.

'First,' quoth he, 'here is my Lord Keeper,
the Bacon hog, the butcher's son, the great
guts, oh he would fry well with a faggot, or
his head would make a fair show upon London
645 Bridge, where I hope shortly it shall stand.
Next is eloquent Master Cecil, Lord Treasurer,
you shall shortly see if he can save his own
life with all the wit he hath; had it not been
for these two before named, England had
650 gone to wrack long since. Then here is the
Earl of Leicester, the Queen's ostler, and his
brother Ambrose Dudley, a good fat whoreson
to make bacon of', with other words of my
Lord of Leicester, not here to be rehearsed.
655 'My Lord of Bedford, he forsooth is the
Queen's cousin: we will see how finely his
cousin and he can hang together. Sir Francis

641-3. *my Lord . . . guts*] Sir Nicholas Bacon, 1509-79,
Lord Keeper of the Great Seal from 1558 and Privy Councillor. He was a 'butcher's son' because his father, Robert Bacon
of Drinkstone, Suffolk, had been sheep-reeve to the abbey of
Bury St. Edmunds.

643. *faggot*] bundle of wood, here in reference to the
burning of heretics; but also a comestible made out of a pig's
guts, and fried. The *O.E.D.*'s earliest reference for the latter
sense, however, is 1851.

644-5. *his . . . Bridge*] Heads of criminals were affixed to
the top of Bridge Gate; and the 'boar's head' was a dish introduced with great ceremony at feasts.

646. *Master Cecil*] William Cecil, 1520-98, Elizabeth's
chief minister.

650. *gone to wrack*] and ruin, presumably—an odd view
for the priest to have. It sounds more like Munday, who may
also intend a play on the word 'rack'.

651. *the Queen's ostler*] Robert Dudley was created
Master of the Horse soon after Elizabeth's accession.

652. *Ambrose Dudley . . . whoreson*] 1528?-90, Earl of
Warwick, and Privy Councillor 1573. His first marriage made
him the son-in-law of William Whorwood—thus 'whoreson'.

655. *Lord of Bedford*] Francis Russell, 1527?-85, Earl of
Bedford, and Privy Councillor from 1558. Any English nobleman might be addressed as 'cousin' (l. 656) by Elizabeth,
although there may be a suggestion here that Russell and
Elizabeth were on particularly intimate terms. Certainly he
was one of her favourites.

657-8. *Sir Francis Walsingham*] 1530?-90, head of the

Walsingham and Doctor Wilson, they be her
Secretaries: for every warrant they have suffered, to apprehend any of our priests, our   660
friends, or other, by that time they have
counted their reckoning, they shall find they
have a dear payment. Sir Christopher Hatton,
he pleased the Queen so well, dancing before
her in a masque, that since that time he hath   665
risen to be one of the Council', with other
words, which I refer for modesty. Sir Francis
Knollys, and other of the Council whose
names I well remember not, he gave them
many a heavy threatening. Then opening the   670
paper farther, at the end thereof was a great
many of names, of magistrates and other
belonging to this city, among whom was
Master Recorder, Master Nowell Dean of
Paul's, Master Foxe, Master Crowley, and   675

*Everyone that was
named in the paper,
the manner and
order of their death
was appointed.*

secret service from 1569 and Secretary of State from 1573.

658. *Doctor Wilson*] Thomas Wilson, 1525?-81, author
of *The Art of Rhetoric* (1553), Privy Councillor and Secretary
of State from 1578.

663-6. *Sir Christopher Hatton . . . Council*] Hatton,
1540-91, in fact rose even higher, becoming Lord Chancellor
in 1587. An accomplished dancer, he acted in the masque at
the Inner Temple revels, Christmas 1561. This, the so-called
'great masque', was taken to court on 18 Jan. 1562, and
Hatton's dancing attracted Elizabeth's attention. Thereafter
their relationship grew increasingly intimate. See Eric St.
John Brooks, *Sir Christopher Hatton* (London, 1946), pp.
36-9.

667. *refer*] reserve.

667-8. *Sir Francis Knollys*] 1514?-96, Privy Councillor
from 1558.

670. *threatening*] warning of injury.

674. *Master Recorder*] William Fleetwood, 1535?-94,
Recorder (magistrate with criminal and civil jurisdiction) of
London from 1571 and M.P. for London. Fleetwood was
particularly vigorous against vagrants and Catholics.

674. s.n. order of 2: order of of 1.

675. *Master Foxe*] John Foxe, 1516-87, Canon of Salisbury, 1563, and author of *Acts and Monuments* (1563)—'The
Book of Martyrs'.

675. *Master Crowley*] Robert Crowley, 1518?-88, Archdeacon of Hereford, 1559, Prebendary of St. Paul's, 1563,
and vicar at St. Lawrence Jewry 1576-8.

sundry other, whose names I cannot very well remember, and therefore am loath to set down anything but that whereof I am certainly assured: but very well I remember there was 680 no one named but he had the order of his death appointed, either by burning, hanging, or quartering, and such like.

It is not unlike but that this unreverent matter will offend some in the reading, that 685 men of honour and worship, and those of credit and countenance, should have their names published in print in such sort; I have had the judgement of those of worship and learning on this behalf, and they have said 690 how it is necessary that their own wicked speeches should be set down for an example to all men, how they abuse Her Majesty, her Honourable Council, and learned and discreet magistrates, whereby their traitorous dealings 695 may be the better discovered. And to them thus undutifully regarded, it cannot seem an offence, considering that Christ unto his

Matthew 5.11.

chosen vessels hath said, 'You shall be mocked, scorned, and reviled for my sake: 700 but do you rejoice and be glad, for your reward is the greater in the Kingdom of Heaven, and you remain blessed.'

Then putting up his paper again, he began after this manner: 'As I have said before, so 705 now I say the same, such as come to his holy place must faithfully bend his life and conversation to honour and reverence our provident and Holy Father the Pope in all things that shall like him to command, to hold and con- 710 fess him the universal supreme head of Christ's Church, and embrace his decrees as the only

There are other here, to whom the like charge hath been given, to justify that I do not report any untruth.

685. *honour and worship*] worth and high standing.
686. *credit and countenance*] here practically synony-mous—repute, estimation.
693. *discreet*] judicious.

ordinance and will of God. For he is the
person of God on earth, and he cannot sin,
because the spirit of divine grace guideth him
continually; he hath authority over all kings 715
and princes to erect and suppress whom he
pleaseth, and that shall England well know
ere long, that he hath such power and authority. To honour and obey him, to be a true and
faithful member of his Church, and to live 720
and die in his cause, this ought to be the
intent of all that cometh here.'

This long tale, containing a number of
more circumstances than I can unfold, made
me study what answer I should make him, 725
which after some pause, came forth as thus:
'Credit me sir, I am but a novice in these
matters, and therefore you might as well have
disputed with me in the deepest schoolpoints
that is, and I should have censured both alike.' 730

'Nay,' quoth he, 'I think not your ignorance
so great, albeit it seemeth great enough,
though you have been loosely brought up,
yet you have been with me, both at mass and
at confession divers times, at such time as I 735
served my Lady B. Beside, there are a great

A number of places
he told me here in
England,   where
priests have enter-
tainment.

712-15. *he is . . . continually*] The priest might well have
claimed that the Pope is the Vicar of Christ, or God's repre-
sentative on earth, that he is guided by 'the spirit of divine
grace', that he is the divinely appointed defender of Christian
faith and morals, but hardly that 'he is the person of God on
earth', unless by 'person' is meant 'parson'. The fact that
Popes have confessors disposes of the proposition that the
Pope cannot sin. Munday, or the priest, may be blurring the
distinction between the man and the office. Perhaps what the
priest meant was that normally sinful acts (killing Elizabeth,
for example) can be good acts if the Pope says so.

716-18. *to erect . . . long*] In fact Pius V had already ex-
communicated Elizabeth in the bull *Regnans in Excelsis*
(1570) and, theoretically, deposed her, releasing English
Catholics from their allegiance. The priest has in mind a right
to the use of force.

729. *schoolpoints*] fine points of scholastic philosophy
debated in the universities.

730. *censured*] given an opinion of.

many of priests in England, as in Warwick-
shire, at Master I. T. in Staffordshire, at
Master G. of C. and at S. T. F. in the same
740 shire: all these be near your father's, and not
one of them but visiteth your father's house
three or four times every year, as they did
when I was there (for there is no long tar̞ri-
ance in one place for a priest, but he must
745 shift still, lest he be taken), and I am sure
your father would see you duly confessed.'

Now I was put to so hard a shift, that I
knew not well what to say, I knew none of
these men he named but one, and he indeed
750 had a priest, who after his long ranging about
his master the Pope's business here in England
I thank God I have caused to be stayed. Likewise, I knew not the gentleman whom both
they at Paris, and he, said to be my father,
755 neither where he dwelt, nor what he was:
which made me stand in fear to be disproved,
having avouched myself before to be his son.

It was only God
that framed my
answers to agree
with the priest's
demands.

Wherefore, referring my case to God, who had
so provided for me till that time, in his name I
760 resolved myself on this answer, not knowing
how it might happen to speed.

An excuse serving
very fit for my pur-
pose, and liked the
priest well enough.

'Indeed sir, I cannot deny but that I have
oftentimes heard mass, as also been at confession, but my devotion thereto hath been
765 slender, as you yourself have seen, knowing
me to be so wild and, as it were, without

739. *Master G. of C.*] possibly the recusant John Gifford,
esq., of Chillington in Staffordshire, who appears in *Recusant
Roll No. 1, 1592-3, C.R.S.* xviii (1916), 295-6.

739. *S. T. F.*] almost certainly Sir Thomas Fitzherbert of
Staffordshire. Although he spent much of his life in prison,
his house evidently remained a safe harbour for, among
others, Robert Persons and Anthony Babington. See, e.g.,
C.S.P.Dom. 1581-90, p. 365, and *C.R.S. Miscellanea*, viii
(1913), 93.

747. *shift*] Munday is playing on the word, which he has
just used in another sense.

761. *speed*] succeed.

government; but when you departed from
my father's, I tarried there but a small time
after you, for I obtained leave of my father to
go lie at London, at a kinsman's house of his, 770
because I would study the French tongue, to
have some knowledge therein against I went
over, for my father told me long before that I
should go to Paris and study there. When I
was at London I grew in acquaintance with 775
divers gentlemen, in whose company I frequented many delightful pastimes, so that I
could hardly refrain them when my father
sent for me, to the intent I should travel to
Paris.'   780

'Well,' quoth he, 'and though you did go to
London so soon after I was gone, any of the
priests that resorted to your father's, or he
himself, could have certified you of such
places in London where you might have heard 785
mass, and been confessed too, without suspect
at all. For at Master S. his house on the backside of P. you might divers times have heard
mass, and been confessed there likewise; I lay
there an indifferent while, and said mass there, 790
whereat divers were present, also in the afternoon when they have been at the play, in all
that time I have confessed many.

'Likewise, you might have gone to the
Marshalsea and enquired for Master Pounde, 795

A matter worthy to
be regarded.

772–3. *against I went over*] in anticipation of my going
over.
777. *pastimes*] entertainments.
778. *refrain*] refrain from.
787–8. *on the backside of P.*] behind St. Paul's presumably.
790. *an indifferent while*] a moderate time.
792. *when . . . play*] the afternoon was the usual time for
performances in the public theatres (or inn-yards before
1576). It is just possible that by 'play' is meant gambling.
794–5. *the Marshalsea*] a London prison in Southwark.
As the context makes clear, imprisonment there did not
necessarily mean close confinement.
795. *Master Pounde*] Thomas Pounde, 1538?–1612?, left

Everard Duckett was taken going into the Marshalsea, to speak with the papists, he being a priest; and being there taken, behaved himself in such traitorous manner that he was executed at Tyburn, 1581.

and you should seldom have missed,-but have found a priest there with him: for sometime under the habits of gentlemen, servingmen, or what apparel they imagine most convenient
800 for them, priests do daily resort unto him, where they confess him and give him such hallowed things as are sent him from Rome, as *Agnus Dei*s, *grana benedicta*, and other things; there, if you had made him privy to
805 your intent, he would have appointed one that should have done it for you. He likewise would have bestowed on you some of those holy things, for he findeth such means, what with the priests that come to him, and other,
810 whom he hireth or entreateth to carry a letter abroad now and then for him, that those holy things are delivered to their hands, who do not a little rejoice in them. Myself once made Norris the pursuivant carry a letter for me, to
815 one of my Lady B. her gentlewomen, and therein was two *Agnus Dei*s, a hallowed girdle, and above forty or fifty *grana benedicta*, which maketh me to smile every time I think

Elizabeth's court in 1569 after she publicly insulted him, converted to Catholicism, and became a Jesuit lay brother in 1578. In 1581 he was transferred from the Marshalsea, in which he had spent much of the 1570s, and imprisoned in the Tower, where he was interrogated on his association with Edmund Campion. See *A.P.C.* xiii (1581-2), 170, 172, 176.

797. s.n. *Everard Duckett*] Everard Hanse, or Haunce, d. 1581, went to Reims and was ordained 1581, returning to England under the pseudonym Evans Duckett. He was arrested while visiting prisoners in the Marshalsea, and executed on 31 July 1581.

803. Agnus Deis] 'lambs of God'; wax medallions carrying the figure of a lamb and blessed by the Pope.

803. grana benedicta] 'hallowed grains'; rosary beads blessed by the Pope.

814. *Norris the pursuivant*] a government messenger hardly noted for his Catholic sympathies. See Richard Challoner, *Memoirs of Missionary Priests*, ed. J. H. Pollen (London, 1924), pp. 86, 112.

815. Lady B. her 2: Lady B. *1*.

816. *girdle*] presumably the cord tied around the alb worn by clerics.

on it, that I could make him my man, when I
durst not deliver it myself.'   820

Master Norris being told this, offereth his
life if any such thing can be proved, for he
sayeth he never delivered anything to any of
my Lady B. her gentlewomen. And for his
faithful service to Her Majesty, I have to show   825
under his own hand the penalty he putteth
himself to, if any unjust service can be laid to
his charge.

By this time the bell rung for all the students to come to supper, which made the   830
priest to stay at this *periodus*, else he would
have continued in discourse I know not how
long: for what with the several charges wherewith he sounded me, my care still how to
shape a sufficient answer, and the tediousness   835
of his tale, mixed with so many words, far
distant from civil and dutiful regard, he was
not so ready to go to his supper, as I was glad
for that time to break off company.

So after certain familiar behaviour used   840
between him and I, he glad to see me at
Rome, and well hoping in short time to make
me a new man, I appliable with thanks for
everything, for that it stood with wisdom to
accept all things: he went into the *refector-*   845
ium, which is the name of their dining hall,
and I to the chamber appointed for me and
my fellow, whom I found there sitting with
Doctor Morris, staying my coming, that we
might sup together, which indeed we did,   850
Master Morris using us very courteously,
passing away the supper-time with much
variety of talk, among which Master Doctor

831. *periodus 2*: *periadus 1*; completed sentence.
833. *charges*] (implied) accusations.
843. *appliable*] docile.
845. things 2: thing *1*.
849. *staying*] awaiting.

said his pleasure of divers persons in England:
855 which, for that it would rather check modesty
than challenge any respect of honesty, I admit
it to silence, the talk being so broad that it
would stand as a blemish to my book.

---

854. *said his pleasure*] said whatever he pleased.
857. *broad*] outspoken.

In what manner our Englishmen pass away their time in the College, the orders of 860 the house, and other things to be regarded.

CHAPTER 3

It is unpossible for me to note down half the speeches that passed between the scholars and me, as also my fellow; but as for that was 865 used to him, I could seldom come acquainted withal, except I had stood by and heard it, for either they had fully persuaded him, or he joined into consent with them, so that he would never report anything that had passed 870 between them, he liked so well of everything. But letting these matters pass awhile, I think it expedient here to set down before I go any farther the orders used in the English College, how the Englishmen spend the time there, 875 and within what compass they limit themselves, which so briefly as I can, I will pass over.

The English College is a house both large and fair, standing in the way to the Pope's Palace, not far from the Castel Sant'Angelo; 880 in the College the scholars are divided by certain number into every chamber, as in some four, in some six, or so many as the rector thinketh convenient, as well for the health of the scholars, as the troubling not 885 much room. Every man hath his bed proper to himself, which is two little trestles, with four or five boards laid along over them, and thereon a quilted mattress, as we call it in England, which every morning after they are risen, they 890 fold up their sheets handsomely, laying them in the midst of the bed, and so roll it up to

The place where the English College standeth in Rome.

The order for the Englishmen's lodging.

880. *Castel Sant'Angelo*: Castle *Sante Angelo* 1.

one end, covering it with the quilt that is their coverlet all the night-time.

895 First in the morning, he that is the porter of the College ringeth a bell, at the sound whereof every student ariseth and turneth up his bed, as I have said before. Not long after, the bell ringeth again, whenas everyone 900 presently kneeling on his knees, prayeth for the space of half an hour, at which time, the bell being tolled again, they arise and bestow a certain time in study, every one having his desk, table and chair to himself very orderly, 905 and all the time of study, silence is used of everyone in the chamber, not one offering molestation in speech to another.

The time of study expired, the bell calleth them from their chambers down into the 910 *refectorium*, where every one taketh a glass of wine and a quarter of a manchet, and so he maketh his *collatione*. Soon after, the bell is knolled again, whenas the students two and two together walk to the Roman College, 915 which is the place of school or instruction, where every one goeth to his ordinary lecture, some to divinity, some to physic, some to logic, and some to rhetoric. There they remain the lecture-time, which being done, they 920 return home to the College again, where they spend the time till dinner, in walking and talking up and down the gardens.

907. *molestation*] annoyance.
911. *manchet*] roll of very fine wheaten bread.
912. collatione] a light repast taken by the members of a religious institution such as this—here obviously not as in *O.E.D.* Collation, sb., 8, 'at close of day', but as in modern Italian, *prima collazione*, breakfast.
914. *the Roman College*] the Collegium Romanum, founded by St. Ignatius Loyola in 1551. It rapidly gained the status of a university, was expanded by Gregory XIII, and was thereafter increasingly referred to by its present name, the Gregorian University—*Pontificia Università Gregoriana*.
916. *ordinary*] regular, appointed.
917. *physic*] medicine.

And an order there is appointed by the rector and the Jesuits, and obeyed by all the students, that whosoever doth not in the 925 morning turn up his bed handsomely, or is not on his knees at prayer-time, or heareth not mass before he go to school, or after he comes home, but forgetteth it; or else if he go forth, and put not the peg at his name in the 930 table. For there is a table hangeth by the door, which hath a long box adjoined to it, wherein lieth a great company of wooden pegs, and against the name of every scholar written in the table (which is observed by order of the 935 alphabet) there is a hole made wherein such as have occasion to go abroad must duly put a peg, to give knowledge who is abroad and who remaineth within.

Beside, divers other orders they have for 940 slight matters, the neglecting whereof is public penance at dinner-time; whenas all the students are placed at the tables, such as have so transgressed, goeth up into the pulpit (which standeth there, because one readeth all the 945 dinner-time) and there he sayeth, 'Because I have not fulfilled this or that', whatsoever order it be that he hath broken, 'I am adjoined such a penance.' Either to kneel in the midst of the hall on his bare knees, and there to say 950 his beads over; or to say certain paternosters, and Ave Marias; or to stand upright and have a dish of pottage before him on the ground, and so to bring up every spoonful to his mouth, or to lose either one or two or three 955

The diversity of penance adjoined the English students, which they do openly in the hall, at dinner-time.

All these I have been forced to do, albeit it were with an ill will.

923–31. *And . . . table*] perhaps the most flagrantly ungrammatical sentence in *E.R.L.*
923. s.n. *adjoined*] enjoined.
924. *the Jesuits*] Three Jesuits were superintending the studies, and thus had a say in directing the College, at this time. See the letter of Gregory Martin to Edmund Campion, 13 Feb. 1579, in *Records of the English Catholics under the Penal Laws (Douay Diaries)*, ed. T. F. Knox (London, 1878), i. 319.

of his dishes appointed for his dinner; or to stand there all dinner-time, and eat no meat; and divers other, which according as it is, either afterward he hath his dinner or
960 supper, or else goes without it. And all these penances I have been forced to do, for that I was always apt to break one order or other. As for the private penances, it shall not be greatly amiss to rehearse them here too: so
965 long I shall desire you to stay from hearing the manner of the students' dinner. The private penances are appointed by the ghostly father at confession, which are fulfilled without public knowledge of the cause, and like-
970 wise of the person. If his penance be to whip himself openly in the hall at dinner-time, then the rector ordereth it after this manner, that he shall not be known, to be reproached by any of his fellows, or that they shall certainly
975 say, it is such a one. At the dinner or supper that this penance is to be accomplished, the rector causeth seven or eight to keep their chambers, and commonly but one that time in a chamber; their doors must be made fast
980 to them, and they not so much as look out at their window, to see from which chamber he comes that doth the penance. When they are all set at the tables, he cometh in, clothed in a canvas vesture down to the ground, a hood
985 of the same on his head, with two holes wherethrough he hath sight, and a good big round place bare, against the midst of his back. In this order he goeth up and down the hall, whipping himself at that bare place, inso-
990 much that the blood doth trickle on the ground after him. The whip hath a very short

The private penances, which are appointed by the ghostly father.

The whipping themselves publicly at dinner.

958. *meat*] food.
962. always *2*: alway *1*.
967–8. *ghostly father*] father confessor.

handle, not much above a handful long, and
forty or fifty cords at it, about the length of
half a yard, with a great many hard knots on
every cord, and some of the whips hath 995
through every knot at the end crooked wires,
which will tear the flesh unmercifully.

The Jesuits have, some of them, to whip
themselves, whips with cords of wire, wherewith they will beat themselves till with too 1000
much effuse of blood they be ready to give
up the ghost. And this they will do in their
chambers, either before a crucifix or the
image of Our Lady, turning their backs when
they bleed toward the image, that it may see 1005
them. One of the Jesuits, because they could
never get me to whip myself (for that I well
knew God said, 'Rent your hearts, and not
your skin', and that 'A contrite and sobbing
heart is more acceptable to God than a bleed- 1010
ing body'), took me once with him into his
chamber, saying I should see (because I was so
fearful) what he would inflict upon his own
body. So when he was unapparelled, he took
a whip, the cords whereof was wire, and before 1015
the picture of Our Lady, he whipped himself
very grievously, saying, '*Sancta Maria Mater
Dei, suscipe dolorem meum; Sancta Maria
Mater Dei, accipe flagitium meum; et ora pro
me, nunc et in hora mortis*', which is as much 1020
to say, 'St. Mary Mother of God, receive my
dolour; St. Mary Mother of God, accept my
whipping; and pray for me, now and in the
hour of death.' These, with other like
words, he used to the picture a great many 1025
times, and then he went to the crucifix which
stood upon his desk, and whipping himself

The manner of the
Jesuits' whips
wherewith they
whip themselves.

Joel 2.13.
Psalm 51.17.

The example one
of the Jesuits gave
me, to whip my-
self.

O monstrous ig-
norance.

992. *handful*] four inches.
1001. *effuse*] effusion.
1008-11. *Rent . . . body*] Munday subtly alters the texts
he cites to make them more relevant to his purposes.

still, he said these, or the very like words: '*O
Iesu, obtestetur te virgo gloriosa Maria mater,*
1030 *quae (quod pro certo novi) pro me nunc
tecum agit. Flagitii tui, sanguinolenti tui
sudoris, crucis tuae, mortis ac passionis tuae,
pro me passae memoria, ad hoc me faciendum
impulit: eo quod perpessus sis, his decies pro
1035 me graviora*', in English thus, 'O Jesus, be
thou entreated by that glorious virgin thy
mother, who I am sure at this time maketh
intercession to thee for me. The remembrance
of thy whipping, bloody sweat, cross, death
1040 and passion, maketh me do this, insomuch as
thou hast suffered ten times more for me.'

In these and suchlike acclamations, he continued whipping himself almost the space of
half an hour, bleeding so sore as it grieved me
1045 very much to see him. Afterward, he willed
me to try it once, and I should not find any
pain in it but rather a pleasure. 'For,' quoth
he, 'if Christ had his flesh rent and torn with
whips, his hands and feet nailed to the cross,
1050 his precious side gored with a lance, his head
so pricked with a crown of thorn, that his
dear blood ran trilling down his face, and all
this for you, why should you fear to put your
body to any torment, to recompense him that
1055 hath done so much for you?' I desired him to
bear with me a while, for I was not endued
with that strength and fortitude as to abide
and suffer the pains he did, but yet in time I
doubted not to fulfil anything on my body he
1060 would command me. My answer pleased him
indifferently, so I left him in his chamber and
went down, lamenting to see a spectacle of so
great folly.

1044. *sore*] severely.
1052. *trilling*] flowing (rather than trickling).
1056. *endued*] endowed.

Now as for the other penances, as they be
divers, so be they divers ways fulfilled, either
by fasting, wearing a shirt of hair, trudging
to the seven churches, lying upon the bare
boards, going into the dark vaults under the
ground, or travelling on pilgrimage, and a
number more, which exceedeth my memory
to unfold, they have amongst them, as there
be divers can bear me witness, and some of
them my confessor hath constrained me to do.

1065 *Diversity of penances given them all by their ghostly confessor.*

1070

Return we now to the students, who being
come from the schools and having recreated
themselves somewhat, either in the house or
in the gardens, are now at the sound of the
bell come into the *refectorium* to dinner. The
custom is that daily two of the students take
it by turns to serve all the other at the table,
who to help them, have the butler, the porter,
and a poor Jesuit, that looketh to all the
scholars' necessaries, to bring them their clean
shirts, and foreseeth that neither their gowns,
cassocks, doublets, breeches, hose nor shoes
want mending. These bring in their hands
each of them a round board which hath a staff
about half a yard long made fast through the
middle of it; and round about that board is
set little saucers, wherein the cook shareth
every man a little quantity, which they bring
and hold over the table, whenas every man
taketh his own mess.

1075

The manner of the Englishmen's dinner.

1080

1085

1090

As for their fare, trust me it is very fine and
delicate, for every man hath his own trencher,
his manchet, knife, spoon and fork laid by it,

1095 *The variety of dishes and daintiness of the Englishmen's fare.*

1067. *the seven churches*] see the following chapter.
1068. *the dark vaults*] the catacombs, described in Chapter Five. See note to l. 1618 below.
1075. having 2: have *1*.
1075. *recreated*] refreshed.
1093. *mess*] serving of food.
1095. *delicate*] delicious.
1095. *trencher*] platter.

and then a fair white napkin covering it, with his glass and pot of wine set by him. And the first mess, or *antepast* as they call it, that is
1100 brought to the table is some fine meat to urge them have an appetite: as sometime the Spanish anchovies, and sometime stewed prunes and raisins of the sun together, having such fine tart syrup made to them as I promise you
1105 a weak stomach would very well digest them. The second is a certain mess of pottage of that country manner, no meat sod in them, but are made of divers things, whose proper names I do not remember: but methought
1110 they were both good and wholesome. The third is boiled meat, as kid, mutton, chicken, and suchlike: every man a pretty modicum of each thing. The fourth is roasted meat, of the daintiest provision that they can get, and
1115 sometime stewed and baked meat, according as pleaseth Master Cook to order it. The fifth and last is sometime cheese, sometime preserved conceits, sometime figs, almonds and raisins, a lemon and sugar, a pomegranate, or
1120 some such sweet gear: for they know that Englishmen loveth sweetmeats.

And all the dinner-while one of the scholars, according as they take it by weekly turn, readeth: first a chapter of their Bible, and
1125 then in their *Martirilogium* he readeth the mar-

1099. antepast] *antipasto* is the hors d'oeuvre of an Italian meal.
1100. *meat*] here, as at l. 958 above, food.
1107. *that country manner*] the manner of that country (Italy), rather than 'country-style'.
1107. *meat sod*] boiled meat.
1112. *pretty*] respectable, considerable.
1114. *daintiest*] choicest.
1116. fifth *ed*: fift *1, 2*.
1118. *conceits*] sweetmeats.
1120. *gear*] thing.
1124. *their Bible*] the Vulgate.
1125. Martirilogium] the med. Latin form of martyrology, a book giving accounts of the Christian martyrs and saints.

tyrdom of some of the saints, as St. Francis,
St. Martin, St. Longinus, that thrust the spear
into Christ's side, St. Agatha, St. Barbara,
St. Cecilia, and divers other, among whom
they have imprinted the martyrdom of Doctor 1130
Story, the two Nortons, John Felton and
others, calling them by the name of saints
who were here executed at Tyburn for high
treason.

The dinner done, they recreate themselves 1135
for the space of an hour, and then the bell
calleth them to their chambers where they
stay a while, studying on their lectures given
them in the forenoon; anon the bell summon-
eth them to school again where they stay not 1140
past an hour, but they return home again, and
so soon as they be come in, they go into the
refectorium, and there every one hath his glass
of wine, and a quarter of a manchet again,
according as they had in the morning.   1145

Then they depart to their chambers, from

*They have feeding
enough, four meals
a day.*

1126-9. *St. Francis . . . St. Cecilia*] St. Francis of Assisi,
1181/2-1226, was not of course a martyr as Munday suggests.
Among the possible candidates for Munday's 'St. Martin' is
St. Martin I, d. 655, the last Pope to be venerated as a martyr.
But there were two other St. Martins. St. Longinus, according
to legend, was martyred at Caesarea in 58. St. Agatha was a
virgin martyred in Sicily, date uncertain, but in the sixth century or earlier. St. Barbara was martyred, according to tradition, at the instigation of her father, and St. Cecilia, the
patroness of church music, was martyred in the second or
third century.

1130-1. *Doctor Story . . Felton*] John Story, 1510?-71,
was active against Protestants under Mary and reputedly responsible for the establishment of the Inquisition at Antwerp
in 1565. He was kidnapped for the English government, con-
victed of treason, and executed on 1 June 1571. Christopher
Norton, one of the sons of Richard Norton, 1488?-1588,
whose family was prominent in the Northern Rebellion of
1569, was captured with his uncle, Thomas Norton, and
both were executed in 1570. John Felton was executed on
8 Aug. 1570 for having nailed Pius V's bull excommunicating
and 'deposing' Elizabeth to the gates of the Bishop of London's palace.

Their exercise after supper.

whence at convenient time they are called to exercise of disputation, the divines to a Jesuit appointed for them, and every study to a several Jesuit, where they continue the space of an hour, and afterward till supper-time they are at their recreation.

After supper, if it be in winter-time, they go with the Jesuits and sit about a great fire talking, and in all their talk they strive who shall speak worst of Her Majesty, of some of her Council, of some bishop here, or suchlike: so that the Jesuits themselves will often take up their hands and bless themselves, to hear what abominable tales they will tell them. After they have talked a good while, the bell calleth them to their chambers, the porter going from chamber to chamber and lighteth a lamp in every one: so when the scholars come, they alight their lamps, lay down their beds, and go sit at their desks and study a little till the bell rings, when every one falls on his knees to prayers. Then one of the priests in the chamber, as in every chamber there is some, beginneth the Latin litany, all the scholars in the chamber answering him: and so· they spend the time till the bell rings again, which is for everyone to go to bed.

1148. *exercise of disputation*] formal defence of (theological) questions and theses.
1148. *divines*] divinity students, the majority in the College at this time, under the instruction of the three Jesuits (l.924).
1149. *study*] branch of study.
1150. *several*] separate.
1165. *their lamps*] presumably their desk lamps, since the porter has already lit the rooms.
1170. *some*] one or more. These priests are clearly additional to the three supervising Jesuits.

◄▲ Other matters of our English students in the College, their days of recreation at their 1175 vineyard, their walk to the seven churches, a report of some of the Romish relics, and other things concerning their behaviour.

CHAPTER 4

The English students every third or fourth 1180 day go not to the schools but have access abroad, to sport and delight themselves: sometime they walk to their vineyard, and the Jesuits with them, where they pass away the day in divers disports; what game, what toy 1185 anyone can devise, they altogether in pastime join to perform it.

Another day they go to the seven churches, which according as I remember their names, I will here set them down: St. Peter's, St. Paul's, 1190 St. John Lateran's, S. Maria Maggiore, S. Croce, St. Laurence's, St. Sebastian's. In all these churches there be divers relics which make them haunted of a marvellous multitude of people: whereby the lazy lurden friars that 1195 keep the churches get more riches than so many honest men should do. For either at the coming into the church, or else at the altar

The seven churches in Rome, whereto they go on pilgrimage.

1185. *disports*] diversions.
1185. *toy*] fun, entertainment.
1188-92. *the seven . . . St. Sebastian's*] the seven chief basilicas, a long-established pilgrim circuit. S. Croce is the Church of the Sacred Cross of Jerusalem (or the Sessorian Basilica); St. Laurence's in S. Lorenzo fuori le Mura; St. Sebastian's is S. Sebastiano fuori le Mura, on the Appian Way. The others (the 'major basilicas') are well enough known.
1194. *marvellous*] surprising, with the suggestion here that the crowd is wonder-struck.
1195. *lurden*] worthless.
1196. get *ed*: gets *1, 2*.

where the relics be, there standeth a basin, 1200 and the people cast money therein with very great liberality. And there standeth a friar with a forked stick in his hand, and thereupon

A crafty kind of cozenage whereby the ignorant people are be- 1205 guiled.

he taketh everybody's beads that lays them on the altar, and then he wipes them along a great proportioned thing of crystal and gold, wherein are a number of rotten bones which they make the people credit to be the bones of saints; so wiping them along the outside of this tabernacle, the beads steal a terrible deal 1210 of holiness out of those bones, and God knows, the people think they do God good service in it: O monstrous blindness!

But because every good subject may see into the Romish jugglings, and perceive the 1215 subtlety of Antichrist the eldest child of Hell, I will rehearse some of these relics, as many of them as I can possibly call to my remembrance.

A brief rehearsal of some of the Romish relics,
1220   whereby the Pope deceiveth a number,
and hath good gains, to the maintenance of his pomp.

In St. Peter's Church

The Pope's brazen rock, taken for the 1225 rock Christ spake of.

As we enter into the court before St. Peter's Church, there standeth the form of a rock

1203. s.n. *cozenage*] deception.
1204-05. *a great . . . thing*] a large reliquary.
1214. *jugglings*] deception, trickery.
1215. *Antichrist*] the prince of Christ's enemies, here of course the Pope.
1216. *rehearse*] give an account of.
1216-18. *as many . . . remembrance*] Munday's memory is remarkably good. Where his account disagrees with the much fuller account in Andrea Palladio's *Descritione de le chiese de Roma* (Rome, 1554), this will be noted, as will relics not mentioned in Palladio, though there is no reason to question the existence of these ('& molte altre reliquie' is a common phrase in Palladio).
1225-6. *a rock . . . brass*] not in Palladio.

made of brass, an old and ancient thing, the
which is kept there, that the ignorant people
should believe that to be the rock which Our
Saviour spake of to Peter, whenas upon Peter's
confessing him to be Christ the Son of the 1230
living God, he answered, 'Upon this rock I   Matthew 16.18.
will build my Church', which rock he meant
by himself, and not by Peter. This piece of
brass they make the ignorant to believe to be
that rock, and therefore a number as they go 1235
into the church fall down on their knees and
worship this brazen rock with their prayers.

Going thorough the church, we come to a   The half bodies of
chapel, wherein is an high altar, whereon   Sts. Peter and Paul.
standeth a picture of St. Peter and St. Paul: 1240
within that altar, they say, lieth half the bodies
of these two apostles and saints, and therefore
that altar is daily worshipped.

Coming back again into the church, we   The spear that was
come to a square altar wherein, say they, is 1245 thrust into Christ's
the head of the spear that was thrust into   side, and the hand-
Our Saviour's side; but the point thereof is   kercher wherewith
broken off, and is in another place. And in   he wiped his face
the same altar is the handkercher which Christ   when he carried
wiped his face withal when he carried his cross 1250 his cross.
sweating, and left the perfect print thereof on
the cloth: this is called *Vultus sanctus*. How
this altar is honoured, you shall read more in
the chapter which talketh of the *Flagellante*
night.   1255

What other relics be in this church I certainly know not, but they say there is the
bodies of divers saints whose names because I

1231. s.n. Matthew 16.18 *ed*: Math. 16.16.18 *1*; Ma.
16.16.18 *2*.

1249. *the handkercher*] the headcloth of St. Veronica,
often referred to simply as the veronica.

1257-8. *they say . . . saints*] Palladio mentions the bodies
of nine, the heads of six, the shoulders of two, '& altri corpi
& reliquie de santi'.

cannot remember, I will let pass, because I
will not be found in an untruth.

In St. Paul's Church

In this church, under the high altar, is said to
be the other half of the bodies of Sts. Peter
and Paul: this altar is likewise adored with
marvellous reverence.

Not far from this church there is a place
called *Tre fontana*; at this place they say
St. Paul was beheaded, and when his head
was cut off, it leaped three times, and in those
places where it leapt there sprung up presently
three fountains; there is great devotion likewise used at this place.

In St. John Lateran's Church

As we come first to the little chapels before
the church (wherein, they say, Our Lady hath
been divers times seen and therefore hath left
such holiness there, as they pray there a good
while) there standeth a round pillar of stone,
seeming to be but lately made, and on this
stone, say they, the cock stood and crowed at
what time Peter denied Christ: and therefore
they do use to kiss it, make courtesy to it,
and rub their beads on it.

Near to this stone is a broad gate, being the
entrance into the aforesaid chapels, and on
the one side of this gate there is two round
rings of iron, whereon sometime a gate hath
been hanged, to open and shut: in these rings,
say they, the Jews did stick banners all the

The other half of
Sts. Peter and Paul.

Three leaps of St.
Paul's head made
three fountains.

The stone whereon
the cock crew
when Peter denied
Christ.

The rings wherein
the Jews set their
banners when
Christ was cruci-
fied.

1260

1265

1270

1275

1280

1285

1266. *a place*] a monastery, built on the traditional site
of the martyrdom of St. Paul.

1278. *a round . . . stone*] not in Palladio, but its existence
is verified by other writers, for instance the anonymous
author of *Rome in the Nineteenth Century*, ii (Edinburgh,
1822), 234-5.

1282. *make courtesy*] bow in respect.

1287. *rings of iron*] not in Palladio.

while that Christ was crucified, and therefore 1290
for the holiness of them they will draw their
beads thorough the said rings, and kiss them
when they have so done.

From thence we go to a fair large place, in
the midst whereof standeth a font, wherein, 1295
they say, Constantinus Magnus was christened:
in this font every year on Easter even they do
christen Jews, such as do change to their
religion. For there is a certain place appointed
for sermons, whereat the Jews whether they 1300
will or no must be present, because one of
their own rabbins preacheth to them, to convert them, as himself hath been a great while.

In Rome, the Jews have a dwelling-place
within themselves, being locked in their streets 1305
by gates on either side, and the Romans every
night keepeth the keys; all the day-time they
go abroad in the city, and will buy the oldest
apparel that is, an old cloak, doublet, or hose,
that a man would think not worth a penny, of 1310
the Jews you may have the quantity of four
or five shillings for them. Now, that the Jews
may be known from any other people, every

The font wherein
Constantinus Mag-
nus was christened.

1297-1303. *in this . . . while*] Attendance by Jews at ser
mons, normally delivered by converts, had recently become
mandatory, following publication of Gregory XIII's bull *Vices
eius nos* (1 Sept. 1577). Those who were thought to show
any tendency towards conversion were admitted into the
Casa dei Catechumeni, the House of Catechumens established
by Paul III in 1543, where they received Christian instruction.
After forty days, those who so desired were baptized, Holy
Saturday being a traditional time for this.
    1302. *rabbins*] rabbis.
    1304-16. *In Rome . . . ill-favouredly*] The bull *Cum nimis
absurdum* (Paul IV, 1555) turned the Jewish ghetto into a
virtual prison, the entrances to it being locked at night and
during major holidays. By the terms of the bull, Jews were
restricted in their employment and many were forced to live
by dealing in second-hand wares and old clothes. The men
were compelled to wear the yellow cap Munday mentions,
the women a yellow kerchief. See the *Encyclopaedia Judaica*,
xiv (Jerusalem, 1971), 246-51, and the bibliography for the
Rome entry.

one weareth a yellow cap or hat, and if he go
1315 abroad without it they will use him very ill-
favouredly.

In this order they come to the sermon, and
when any of them doth change his faith he
taketh his yellow cap or hat off from his head,
1320 and throws it away with great violence; then
will a hundred offer him a black cap or a hat,
and greatly rejoice that they have so won him.
All his riches he then must forsake, that goes
to the Pope's use, being one of his shifts; and
1325 to this aforesaid font he is brought, clothed
all in white, a white cap, a white cloak, and
everything white about him, with a holy candle
burning, that he beareth in his hand. Then is
he there baptized by an Englishman, who is
1330 named Bishop Goldwell, sometime the Bishop
of St. Asaph in Wales: he hath this office,
maketh all the English priests in the College,
and liveth there among the Theatines very
pontifically. After the Jews be thus baptized,
1335 they be brought into the church, and there
they see the hallowing of the Paschal, which is
a mighty great wax taper; and then a device,
wherein is enclosed a number of squibs, is shot

Bishop Goldwell 1330 (margin)
baptizeth the Jews (margin)
in Rome. (margin)

Hallowing of the (margin)
Paschal candle. (margin)

1323-4. *All . . . use*] The authorities ensured that the convert's portion of the family possessions would be given to him. They did not, as Munday claims, confiscate his possessions.

1330. *Bishop Goldwell*] Thomas Goldwell, d. 1585, Bishop of St. Asaph 1555-8. He was made superior of the Theatine order at Naples in 1561, attended the Council of Trent in 1562, and became Archbishop (later Cardinal) Borromeo's vicar-general in 1563. From 1574 he acted as Diocesan Bishop of Rome and it would have been in this capacity that he baptized the Jews.

1331. *maketh*] ordains.

1333. *Theatines*] members of an order founded by St. Cajetan in 1524.

1336-7. *the Paschal . . . taper*] traditionally lit on Holy Saturday and extinguished on Ascension Day, and symbolizing the risen Christ.

1338. *squibs*] exploding fireworks.

off, when thorough all the church they then
cry, '*Sic transit gloria mundi*.' From thence 1340
they go to a college which the Pope hath erected for such Jews as in this manner turn to his
religion; there they stay a certain time, and
afterward they be turned out to get their
living as they can, none of their former riches 1345
they must have again, for that goes to the
maintenance of the Pope's pontificality. This
aforesaid font is a holy thing, and there must
prayers be likewise said.

From this font we go up into a fair chapel, 1350
wherein is an altar dedicated to Our Lady, in
gold and sumptuous shows surpassing, and all
about the chapel are hanged little wooden
pictures, tapers, and wax candles, which are
the pilgrims' vows to Our Lady, and there 1355
they leave them to honour her. Here must be
used great devotion.

From thence we go into an old room,
wherein is an old wall standing along in the
midst of this room, and in this wall is three 1360
old doors, having painting on them that is not
very old: thorough one of these doors, they
say, Christ went in to judgement; when he
came back from judgement, he went thorough
the second, and thorough the third to be 1365
whipped; these doors are worshipped every
day.

Our Lady's holy chapel.

The three holy doors.

1339–40. Sic . . . mundi] 'Thus the glory of the world
passes.'
1340–47. *From . . . pontificality*] There was a College of
Neophytes, established in 1575 for converts who desired
admission to a religious order. But Munday is apparently
confusing this with the House of Catechumens, which was in
any case entered before, not after, baptism, and where
instruction was given to intending converts for forty days
prior to their acceptance or refusal of the sacrament. It is
doubtful whether any converts, as distinct from converts who
became priests, were forced to relinquish their property.
Throughout this passage Munday seems to be conflating what
he has heard about two separate institutions.

The holy stairs
that Christ went
up to judgement
on.

From thence we go along thorough an old
gallery, and there is a fair pair of stairs of
1370 stone that cometh up into this gallery, being
in number of steps about four or five and
twenty; up these stairs they say Christ went
to judgement, and as he came back again he
let fall a drop of blood on one of the steps,
1375 over the which place (because the people
with kissing it and rubbing it with their
beads have fretted a deep hole in the stone)
is made a little iron grate. The people must
neither go up nor down these stairs on their
1380 feet, but creep them upon their knees, and on
every step say a paternoster and an Ave Maria:
so that with the number that creep up and
down these stairs daily, they are kept as clean
as the fine houses in London, where you may
1385 see your face in the boards. These stairs have
no small reverence.

The veil of the
temple, that rent
in the midst.

Near to the head of these stairs, on either
side of the gallery, there is in the walls two
half pillars of stone, much like to alabaster,
1390 which they say to be the veil of the Temple
that rent in the midst when Christ yielded up
the ghost; upon these two half pillars they
rub their beads in sign of great devotion.

The pillar that
Christ was whip-
ped at.

Somewhat near to these half pillars there
1395 is a long marble pillar, at which pillar, they
say, Christ was fast bound when he was
whipped in Pilate's hall. This pillar is much
adored.

Some of the milk
of Our Lady's
breasts.

Hard by we go into a little chapel which
1400 hath a very rich and costly altar, wherein they
say to be some of the milk that came out of
Our Lady's breasts, and as yet remaineth pure
and sweet. To this relic is used marvellous
worship.

1380. *creep*] creep up.
1389. alabaster *ed*: alablaster *1, 2*.
1395. *a . . . pillar*] not in Palladio.

And in the same chapel, hard by the door as we come in, there hangeth tied with an iron chain a piece of wood which is crossed every way with divers plates of iron: this piece of wood they name to be a piece of the cross whereon the thief was hanged, to whom Our Saviour said, 'This day thou shalt be with me in Paradise.' To this is given much devotion.

> 1405 A piece of the cross whereon the good thief was hanged.

> 1410

Beneath in the Church

In the church at the high altar there is, as they say, the first shirt that Our Lady made for Christ when he was young.

> 1415 The first shirt that was made for Christ.

In the same altar are the two skulls or scalps of the heads of St. Peter and St. Paul, with the hair as yet on them, which are set in gold and silver very costly.

> The heads of St. Peter and St. Paul.

> 1420

There is also a glass vial which is full, as they say, of the blood of Our Saviour, that ran out of his precious side hanging on the cross: the people when this is shown will take their hands and hold the palms of them toward the glass, and then rub all their face with their hands, with the great holiness they receive from the glass.

> A glass vial full of the blood of Christ.

> 1425

Then there is a piece of Christ's coat without seam, and it is the part of the coat which when it was turned down over his body that he should be whipped, the blood did trickle down upon: and upon this piece of his coat, say they, the blood yet remaineth as fresh as it was the first day when it fell on it. This is a marvellous precious relic too.

> 1430 A piece of Christ's coat with his blood yet fresh on it.

> 1435

1405-13. *And in . . . devotion*] Palladio mentions two pieces of Christ's cross in St. John Lateran, but not this item. However, according to Palladio the church of Santa Croce possessed a piece of the good thief's cross, and Munday may have this in mind.

1430. *Christ's coat*] the seamless scarlet cloak for which the soldiers cast lots, after the crucifixion, rather than tear it.

The chain where-
with St. John was
led to Ephesus.

1440

One of the nails
that nailed Christ
on the cross.

A part of the 1445
crown of thorn.

Likewise there is the whole chain of iron
wherewith St. John the Evangelist was led
bound to Ephesus: this chain is a little old
one, I am sure little above half a yard long.

There is also one of the nails wherewith
Our Saviour Christ was nailed on the cross:
and it hath the blood yet fresh upon it.

And among all the rest, there is a great
portion or quantity of the crown of thorn
wherewith they say Our Saviour was crowned.

Divers other relics there be in that church,
which I cannot now very perfectly remember:
1450 but these I am certain they make the people
believe to be there, for I have stood by among
a multitude of people that come thither to
see them on the day they are shown, and
there have I heard all these named; almost all
1455 the English students can bear me witness, for
I have gone in their company, as it is a custom
and an order among them, to go from church
to church all the Lent time, to the stations as
they call them, and then each day in Lent one
1460 church or other hath their relics abroad to be
seen. And then they tell the people, this is the
relic of such a saint, and this is such a holy
and blessed thing: but they be either covered
with gold, silver, or crystal, so that we cannot
1465 tell whether there be anything within or no,
except it be sometime in a broad crystal tabernacle, and there you shall see a company of
rotten bones, God knows of what they be.

1440. *to Ephesus*] *from* Ephesus *to* Rome, according to
an early tradition deriving from Tertullian, of which Munday
here shows his ignorance.

1442. *one of the nails*] not in Palladio.

1445–6. *a great . . . thorn*] not in Palladio.

1457. *order*] established practice.

1458. *stations*] stations of the cross, at certain churches
at specified times. At each station one performs some act of
devotion, indulgences being granted in return.

1462. *relic ed*: relics 1, 2.

1466. *sometime*] occasionally.

1466–7. *tabernacle*] reliquary.

In S. Maria Maggiore

There is an old rotten crib or manger wherein, say they, Our Saviour lay, between the ox and the ass, when the shepherds came to honour and reverence him. This is a thing highly honoured.

There is likewise Aaron's rod, as they call it, which is in the form of a bishop's staff: a holy relic.

There is also of the hair, that grew on Our Lady's head: this is there reserved richly, and worshipped for a singular relic.

There is the form of a finger in silver, wherein, say they, is the finger of St. Thomas, which he thrust into the side of Christ: this is no simple relic.

There is the point of the head of a spear, which they say to be broken off from the spear that was thrust into Our Saviour's side on the cross: a relic of no small worship.

There is also certain pieces of money, which they name to be of those thirty pence which Judas received when he betrayed his Master, wherewith, after he had hanged himself, they bought a field, called the field of blood. These are relics of great estimation.

There is likewise an old rotten piece of wood, which they make the people to think to be a piece of the cross whereon Christ was

1470 The manger wherein Christ was laid.

1475 Aaron's rod.

Hair of Our Lady's head.
1480

St. Thomas his finger.

1485 The point of the spear that was thrust into Christ's side.

Some of the thirty pence for which 1490 Judas betrayed Christ.

1495 A piece of Christ's cross.

1475. *Aaron's rod*] according to Palladio, in St. John Lateran.

1478. *of*] some of. Palladio notices some hair in St. John Lateran, but not here.

1480. *singular*] rare, precious.

1482. *finger of St. Thomas*] not in Palladio.

1484. *simple*] ordinary.

1485. *point . . . spear*] referred to at ll. 1247–8 above; not in Palladio.

1489. *certain . . . money*] not mentioned by Palladio, who does however notice one of the coins in Santa Croce.

1493. *the field of blood*] the potter's field. See Matt. 27:3-10.

1495-6. *piece of wood*] not in Palladio, who notices similar relics in St. John Lateran.

crucified: to see this relic, the people will come creeping on their knees, and behave themselves with marvellous devoutness.

Thorns of the crown of thorns.

There is also certain of the thorns, which sometime, as they say, were on the crown of thorn wherewith Our Savour Christ was crowned: relics of great authority among them.

In S. Croce

Another of the nails wherewith Christ was nailed.

There is another of the nails, wherewith Christ was nailed on the cross: and as they say, the blood still fresh upon it.

More of Judas' pence.

There is also three or four of the pence which Judas received for the betraying of his Master Christ.

More of the cross.

There is a good big piece of wood, which they likewise say to be a piece of the cross whereon Christ was crucified.

One of the whips wherewith Christ was whipped.

There is a whip, which they report to be one of those whips wherewith Christ was whipped in Pilate's hall. This is a holy and very precious relic.

Relics of saints.

There is a tabernacle of crystal, the pillars thereof are of silver, wherein is divers old rotten bones, which they say to be the bones of saints and holy martyrs.

In St. Laurence's

The stone whereon St. Laurence was broiled.

There is made fast in a wall a great marble stone, about two yards in length and a yard

1501. *certain . . . thorns*] Palladio notices two in Santa Croce but none here.

1507-8. *another . . . cross*] Palladio notes only a nail used to put the inscription on the cross.

1510. *three . . . pence*] Palladio notices none here.

1514. *piece . . . cross*] Palladio again is silent, but Santa Croce was always renowned as a shrine of relics of the Passion and holds three pieces of the cross.

1516. *a whip*] not in Palladio.

1520-3. *a tabernacle . . . martyrs*] Palladio notices a number of bodies, heads, and arms.

in breadth, which is closed in with a grate of
iron: upon this stone, they say, St. Laurence
was broiled. This is a relic much set by.

There also they say to be the gridiron 1530
whereon St. Laurence was broiled: but that I
never saw, therefore I will not make any certain report thereof.

There at the high altar they say the head of
St. Laurence is, which they have set in silver 1535
marvellous costly.

In St. Sebastian's
There under the high altar they say lieth the
body of St. Sebastian, to whose shrine they
offer very much worship. 1540

At all these seven churches there are a number
more relics than I can well remember, which
maketh the people to resort to them almost
daily; and our Englishmen, they are as zealous
in these matters as the best, and believe that 1545
those relics are the very certain things whereof
they bear the name, so great is their blindness
and want of faith.

To these places they trudge commonly
once every week, sometime twice, or as the 1550
Jesuits think it convenient: but when they
have been at these seven churches, and honoured all these paltry relics, they think they
have done a most blessed and acceptable
service to God. 1555

There are relics beside these, at most of the
other churches and chapels, but what they be
I do not as now remember; yet thus much I
can say, that when the station hath been at

The gridiron where-
on St. Laurence was
broiled.

The head of St.
Laurence.

The body of St.
Sebastian.

1529. *much set by*] greatly valued.
1530. *the gridiron*] a piece of it, according to Palladio.
1534-5. *head of St. Laurence*] Palladio mentions the
body.
1559-60. *when . . . St. Apollonia's*] 9 February (the
relevant feast day), according to Palladio's *Le Stationi*

Prayer to St. Apollonia for the toothache.

1560 St. Apollonia's, all the way as we go, the streets are full almost of lame and diseased people who, when they desire an alms of the passers-by, say they will pray to St. Apollonia for their teeth, that she will keep them from the 1565 toothache, or any other pain that may happen to their teeth. This they do, because they report that St. Apollonia being martyred, had all her teeth by violence plucked out of her head; and therefore they imagine that she can 1570 defend anybody from having any pain in their teeth.

Prayer to St. Agatha for women's breasts.

Likewise St. Agatha, whose breasts they say were clipped off with a pair of tongs made red hot in the fire: to her they will pray (if the 1575 people will give them any money) that any woman passing by them, this saint will not suffer her to have any pain in her breasts.

A cunning shift of beggars.

Other of their saints, who had anything ministered by way of torment, either on their 1580 head, arms, body, legs, or feet, because the people shall give them somewhat, these beggars will pray to any of those saints to defend them from pain in any such place of their body.

A commanding beggar.

1585 Now some lazy friar, or some other crafty companion, who will not take so much pains as to beg, but that he will compel the people to give him somewhat, he getteth a pax, and

Indulgenti . . . appended to the *Descritione.* That Munday would have been in Rome on this day adds credibility to the scene he describes.

1563. *St. Apollonia*] virgin and martyr, died by fire in 249. As Munday says, and for the reason he gives, she is invoked against toothache. Jean Fouquet's often reproduced miniature of a performance of the medieval *Martyr de Sainte Appolline* (c. 1460) depicts the gruesome extraction. See, e.g., A. M. Nagler, *A Source Book of Theatrical History* (New York, 1959), p. 54.

1572. *St. Agatha*] martyred, in the circumstances described, before 530, and commemorated on 5 February. Again the date supports Munday as a witness.

1588. *a pax*] a small tablet that can be held in the hand,

every one that cometh by him must make
homage to it, come and kiss it, and give him   1590
some money, ere he go any further. This
fellow standeth as master of the beggars, and
all these knaveries, and an infinite number
more, are our Englishmen so insolent both to
like and allow of.   1595

And now seeing I am among the Pope's
pageants, I will blaze a little more of this
holy hell, that those (to whose hands this
my book shall happen to come, and are by
some of our secret seducing priests anything   1600
moved that way) may behold the egregious
follies and devilish drifts, whereby God is
despised, and men too much wilfully blinded.
So that, turning to the bare and naked truth,
which craveth neither shadow nor any coloured 1605
device, they may vomit up that Antichrist and
his abominable inventions, and cleave only to
that which God himself hath commanded.

---

carrying a representation of the crucifixion, and kissed during
mass.
    1597. *blaze*] make known.
    1602. *drifts*] schemes, devices.
    1605-6. *coloured device*] fair-seeming invention.
    1606. *vomit . . . Antichrist*] For Munday the image was
no doubt appropriate, suggesting as it does the exorcising of
an evil spirit.

(➤ A brief discourse of their dark vaults
1610 underneath the ground, and how they beguile
a number by them. Of the pilgrimage to St.
James in Galicia, to S. Maria di Loreto, to
St. Clare at Mount Falcon, and other places
of like holiness.

1615   CHAPTER 5

Among a number of their inventions, to uphold and maintain their wicked dealings, they
have certain vaults underneath the ground
wherein, they say, how in the time that the
1620 persecuting emperors lived in Rome, the
Christians were glad to hide themselves; and

Mark this, good   there they lived many years, having no food
reader, and think   or nourishment to maintain them, but only
well thereon.   that they were fed by angels. Sometime
1625 Christ himself came amongst them, and he fed
them by his heavenly deity. Whenas he could
not come, but was busied about other affairs,
he sent his mother the Virgin Mary to them.
At other times the archangel Michael, the
1630 angel Gabriel, or one angel or other was still
sent unto them; and saints that were living
on earth came daily and preached to them.
This our Englishmen hath told to me and
other, at divers times: yea, and when they

1618. *vaults*] catacombs. Their existence was gradually
forgotten after the ninth century. From 1432, isolated
excursions into, and unscientific examination of some of
them took place, but not until 1578 was their existence
made generally known, and not until Antonio Bosio, 1576?–
1629, began his investigation was their real significance
understood. Munday's scepticism is thus understandable.

1621-2. *and . . . years*] Although the notion has persisted,
the concept of an underground city of fugitive Christians is
no longer supported by historians.

have seen me to offer doubt of those matters, 1635
they have been ready to swear it to be certain
and true.

At a church there called St. Pancratia there
is a vault, whereinto I have gone with the
Jesuits of the English College and the students; 1640
and there they have showed me in divers places
made on either side in the vault as we go, that
there lay such a saint, and there lay such
another, there they were buried, and none was
there, but they were all saints. Then (having 1645
every one of us a wax light in our hands,
because it is unpossible to see any light in
the vault, and for those lights, the friars that
keep the church must have money, which we
put into a basin, that standeth at the going 1650
down into the vault) they look on the ground
under their feet as they go; and if they chance
to find a bone (as some sure are thrown in of
purpose, to deceive the people) whether it be of
a dog, a hog, a sheep, or any beast, they can tell 1655
presently what saint's bone it was, either St.
Francis, St. Anthony, St. Blaise, or some other
saint that pleaseth them to name. Then must
nobody touch it, without he be a priest, and
it must be brought home for an especial relic: 1660
and thus (saving your reverence) increaseth
the genealogy of the holy relics in Rome.

In this aforesaid vault of St. Pancratia, as
one of the English priests in the College gave
me to understand, there was sometime a 1665

A marvellous his-
tory and one of
the Romish mir-
acles.

1638. *St. Pancratia*] St. Pancratius, on the Via Aurelia,
just outside the city walls.

1656-7. *St. Francis . . . St. Blaise*] St. Francis is an odd
inclusion here. The others are St. Anthony, d. 258?, martyr,
and St. Blaise, d. 316?, bishop and martyr.

1661-2. *and thus . . . Rome*] The sarcasm is understandable in view of the general ignorance on the subject of the
catacombs. Of course, while countless relics had already been
transferred from the catacombs to the churches in the eighth
and ninth centuries, it was precisely here that one might still
expect to discover genuine Christian relics.

Franciscan friar, who having long time lived among his brethren in the monastery, in chastity of life and devoutness in religion, walking one day without Rome, St. Francis appeared to him in his friar's cowl, and calling him by his name, said unto him, 'I know my good brother, thou hast long thus lived in my holy order, and hast obeyed me in everything: therefore I will that thou be no longer a mortal man, but a saint. And from this time forward, thou shalt leave thy cloister, and go to the vault under the church of St. Pancratia, where thou shalt be worshipped of everyone that cometh into the said vault, and to them thou shalt give the bones and relics of holy and blessed saints, which they in their churches shall adore with great reverence; what thou wilt have, shall be done, and what thou wilt not, shall not be done.'

After these words, St. Francis vanished from him, and he went home to the monastery, to tell his brethren what had happened; soon after, with burning tapers and great shows of holiness, they brought him to the vault of St. Pancratia wherein, being entered, they found a seat ready prepared for him, which shined as bright as the sun, so that it dimmed the light of all their tapers: it was like unto the clouds, very thick beset with twinkling stars, and over the head of it, it was covered with a goodly rainbow. Nothing could be seen whereon this seat depended, it neither touched the ground, the top of the vault overhead, nor any part of the wall on either side, therefore it was supported by angels, whom though they could not discern, yet they heard them make very melodious harmony, to welcome this saint to his new seat. Then the friar being bashful, to see such

Mark this.

1670
1675
1680
1685
1690
1695
1700

1697. *depended*] hung or rested.

a glorious seat provided for him, withdrew 1705
himself, as though he were unworthy to sit
therein: but then out of one of the clouds
stretched a hand (which they said to be
Christ's) wherein they saw the fresh bleeding
wound, being pierced thorough with the nail 1710
on the cross, and this hand pulled the friar to
the seat, and placed him very royally therein.
At the sight hereof, all his brethren fell down
and worshipped him, whereupon he delivered
unto every one of them divers holy relics: as 1715
the head of such a saint, and bones of divers
other saints, which was put into his hand to
give them. Some of them for pure zeal would
not depart from him, but stayed there many
years, being fed and nourished by angels; the 1720
other, to look to the good ordering of their
monastery, were forced to depart.

A long time this saint remained in that
vault, and many other that came to him,
whom he daily made saints: so that, as well 1725
on the behalf of this saint, as divers other as
good as he, this vault is worshipped as though
it were a second heaven.

When he had ended this brave notorious
fable, delivered forth with far more reverent 1730
gesture than I can set down, or you imagine,
he said, 'If a man should tell this to the heretics of our country, they would straightway
condemn it as a lie and untruth: so mightily
doth the devil prevail with them, to deface 1735
the daily miracles shown in the Catholic
Church.' Trust me, thought I, I know not
whether they would esteem it for a lie or no:
but I do allow it for one of the notablest lies
that ever I heard in all my life.   1740

O my dear countrymen, think how God
hath given over these men, that repose credit
in such abominable untruths, whereby he is

O horrible and
abominable blas-
phemy.

1729. *brave*] excellent, fine.

robbed of his glory, and the worship which
1745 we ought of duty to give to him is bestowed
on a rabble of rascal relics, a dunghill of most
irksome and noisome smell, and they themselves become spectacles to the world, following the Whore of Rome as her puddle of
1750 accursed filthiness. Their impiety hath pierced
the heavens and offended the Almighty, to
see that his creatures shall thus disdain their
Maker; and therefore, while they are glorying
and triumphing in the midst of their wicked-
1755 ness, he hath thrown them down, accounted
them as bastards and not children, that they
might be an example to us, how to live in his
fear, and how to behave ourselves like
Christians, not to give his honour to stocks
1760 and stones, not to lust after dreams and fan-
tasties of the Devil's invention, but while we
have the light, to walk as becometh the
children of light, to keep ourselves true and
faithful subjects to her by whom we enjoy the
1765 light, and to pray to God, to bless her and us
all, to continue in the light. Amen.

I will set down one discourse more, of
another like miracle, done in another of their
vaults; and then I will trouble you no longer
1770 with such frivolous and foolish stuff, which I
will declare even in the same manner as a priest
of theirs, as yet not taken, yet he is here in
England, told me, when he, I, and two of the
scholars more went into the said vault.

Another strange 1775 Without Rome, about the distance of half
history of a Rom-
ish miracle done in
the vault of St.
Priscilla, without
Rome.
a mile from the city, there is a huge great
vault, which they call St. Priscilla's Grot: and
within this vault, there is a great many of

1749. *the Whore of Rome*] the 'scarlet' woman of Revela-
tion 17.
1759-60. *stocks and stones*] idols and graven images, 'gods
of wood and stone'—*O.E.D.* Stock, sb., I, 1, d.
1777. *St. Priscilla's Grot*] on the Via Salaria Nuova.

several places, turning one this way, another
that way, as in one street there may be divers 1780
streets and lanes, turning every way. So that
when they go into this vault, they tie the end
of a line at the going in, and so go on by the
line, else they might chance to lose themselves,
and so miss of their ever coming out again; or 1785
else if they have not a line, they take chalk
with them, and make figures at every turning,
that at their coming again (being guided by
torchlight, for candles will go out with the
damp in the vault) they may make account 1790
till they get forth; but this is not so ready a
way as by the line.

One day I was desirous to see this vault,
for my fellow Thomas Nowell, in the company
of the Jesuits and the scholars, had been there- 1795
in, and I lying sick in my bed, both he and
they made such a glorious report thereof to
me, what a heavenly place it was, what a
number of saints and martyrs had been buried
there, and what precious relics was daily found 1800
there, that I very much desired to see the
thing whereto they gave such an admirable
praise. For in sooth, my fellow was even all
one with them, his company was required of
everyone, and he as lewd in speeches against 1805
his country as the best: so that I was esteemed
I cannot tell how, they would not misdoubt
me for my parents' sake, and yet they would
give me many shrewd nips. As when they
demanded anything of me, as concerning our 1810
gracious Princess, or any of her Honourable
Council, I should answer, 'Her Majesty, God
bless her', or, 'the Right Honourable, such a
nobleman', of whom they asked me: whereat
they would check me very much, for using 1815
any reverence in naming Her Majesty, or any
of the lords of her Honourable Council.

1779. *several*] different, separate.

I speak not this, good reader, either in pride or bravery.

And this I may say boldly, for that it is true, as God is my witness, that in all the time I was amongst them I neither offered moiety of misordered or undecent speech, either of Her Majesty, or any nobleman in the Court, no, nor so much as thought ill of any of them, notwithstanding the words they used, sufficient (had not God ordered all my doings) to have moved a more staid man than myself to an error. I appeal to God, who knoweth I set down nothing but truth, and to him that is my chiefest enemy, if he can justly report otherwise by me: for I thank God, albeit I were so far from my country, he gave me the grace to consider I was a subject, and I was bound by duty to regard and honour my prince so long as I lived. And because my adversaries object against me, that I went to mass, and helped the priest myself to say mass: so that (say they) who is worst, I am as evil as he. I answer, I did so indeed, for he that is in Rome, especially in the College among the scholars, must live as he may, not as he will; favour comes by conformity, and death by obstinancy.

These rash heads being in England would do many goodly matters at Rome, they would tell the Pope of his lascivious and unchristian life, the cardinals of their sodomitical sins, the friars of their secret juggling with the nuns, and the priests of their painted Purgatory, their wafer God, and their counterfeit blood in the chalice: all this they would do, now they are in England. But I doubt if they were at Rome, and beheld the merciless tyranny executed on the members of Christ, God having not endued them with the spirit of perseverance, to suffer and abide the like (for

The will of God must be done in all things.

1818. s.n. *bravery*] bravado.
1848. *painted*] pretended.

what can this frail carcase endure, if God do
not say, 'I will that thou shalt suffer this'?),
I fear me, they would be as ready to do anything for the safeguard of their lives as I was.
You may note a special example in these our   1860
countrymen lately executed, that neither
their cause was esteemed of God, nor perfectly
persuaded in themselves; yet they would die
in a bravery, to be accounted martyrs at
Rome, and in the midst of their bravery, all   1865
the world might note their false and faint
hearts.

Sherwood, he ran down the ladder when
death should arrest him, having killed one of
his fellow papists. Campion, their glorious cap-   1870
tain, he looked dead in the face so soon as he
saw the place of execution, and remained
quaking and trembling unto the death. Shert
would have the people think he feared not
death, and yet he catched hold on the halter   1875
when the cart was drawn away. Kirby, quaking

1865. *bravery*] display of courage.
1868. *Sherwood*] not the martyr Thomas Sherwood,
1551?-78, but William Sherwood, d. 1581?, a Catholic who
killed a fellow prisoner. See the anonymous *A True Report
of the Late Horrible Murder Committed by W. Sherwood*
(1581). This is just possibly by Munday. It was entered to
Charlewood on 17 July 1581.
1870. *Campion*] Edmund Campion, 1540?-81, the most
renowned of the English Jesuit martyrs, was made an Anglican
deacon in 1564 but later reconciled himself to Catholicism,
fleeing to Douai in 1571. He became a Jesuit and taught in
Prague where he was ordained, 1578. In 1580 he embarked
with Robert Persons on the first Jesuit mission to England,
where his success was astounding. Following his capture he
suffered cruel examinations and torture directed at securing
a confession of treasonable activity. On 20 Nov. 1581 Munday
was a witness against Campion, whom he did not know, and
others whom he had met—Henry Orton, Ralph Sherwin, and
Luke Kirby. Campion was executed with Ralph Sherwin and
Alexander Briant on 1 Dec. 1581; all three were canonized in
1970. Munday is obviously untrustworthy on the way
Campion and the others faced their deaths.
1873. *Shert*] John Shert was sent on the English mission
in 1579, and executed on 28 May 1582.
1876. *Kirby*] Luke Kirby studied at Douai and Rome,

when he felt the cart go away, looked still
how near the end of it was, till he was quite
beside. And Cottam dismaying, died trembling
1880 and in great fear. These are the marytrs of the
Romish Church, not one of them patient,
penitent, nor endued with courage to the
extremity of death, but dismaying, trembling
and fearful, as the eyewitnesses can bear me
1885 record. We may therefore well know that a
good cause doth animate the martyr, which
belonging to God, let Rome, Hell, and all the
devils set themselves against us, they can touch
us no farther than God will suffer them. As

St. Laurence.   1890 St. Laurence being broiled on the gridiron, to
witness the invincible courage wherewith God
endued him, he said, 'Thou tyrant, this side is
now roasted enough, turn the other.' And St.

St. Isidore.   Isidore likewise said to the tyrant, 'I know
1895 thou hast no further power over me, than my
God will suffer thee from above.' But now to
our matter.

As I have said, through the great report
they made of this vault, one of the priests,
1900 two of the scholars and I, took with us a line,
and two or three great lights, and so we went
to this aforesaid vault; we going along in
farther and farther, there we saw certain
places one above another, three and three on

---

was sent on the English mission in 1580, and was executed
on 30 May 1582 (canonized 1970). His kindnesses to Munday
while both were in Rome are admitted by Munday in the *Brief
and True Report, of the Execution of Certain Traitors* (1582).

1879. *beside*] beside himself.

1879. *Cottam*] Thomas Cottam, 1549-82, studied at
Douai and Rome, ordained a Jesuit at Reims, and sent on the
English mission in 1580. Executed on 30 May 1582, with
Kirby and two others.

1890. *St. Laurence*] roasted to death in 258.

1893-4. *St. Isidore*] of Chios, martyred in 251?

1903-07. *certain . . . martyrs*] The detail here enforces
the fact of Munday's visit to the catacombs. See, e.g., the first
illustration on p. 395 in Vol. ix of the *Enciclopedia italiana*
(Rome, 1949).

either side, during a great way in length: and 1905
these places they said to be some of them the
graves of persecuted saints and martyrs, where
they hid themselves in the time of the cruel
emperors of Rome, and there they died.

Proceeding on forward, we came to an old 1910
thing like an altar, whereon, in old and ancient
painting (which was then almost clean worn
out) was Christ upon the cross, and Our Lady
and St. John by him; there, the priest said, St.
Peter, St. Paul, and many other saints, had 1915
said mass to the Christians that hid themselves
there. 'And besides this,' quoth he, 'there
chanced not many years since, a poor man of
the city to come into this vault, and when he
was come so far as this altar, the light he 1920
carried in his hand suddenly went out, so
that he was forced to sit down, and stay here.
He being thus without any light, and ignor-
ant of the way to get out again, fell in prayer   A strange and rare
to Our Lady, who presently appeared to him, 1925   miracle,   too
having about her little angels, holding burning   strange to be true.
lamps in their hands, wherethrough the place
was illumined very gloriously. And there she
questioned with him, and he with her, about
many holy and religious matters: then she 1930
departing left him there accompanied with
angels, so that he remained there ten days, at
the end whereof he came forth and went and
told the Pope what he had seen, for which,
when he died, he was canonised a saint, and in 1935
this order arise many of our Romish saints.'

1911-14. *an altar . . . him*] The image is either a late
'addition' to the art of the catacomb of Priscilla or, less probably, Munday's memory fails him. This catacomb contains
what is thought to be the earliest portrayal of the Blessed
Virgin Mary, with the Christ child (early third century).
However, there are no known Christian representations of
the crucifixion antedating the fifth century, and the picture
Munday describes suggests a still later date. See the articles
on 'Crucifixion (In Art)' and 'Mary, BV, Iconography of' in
the *New Catholic Encyclopedia* (New York, 1967), iv. 486 ff.
and ix. 369.

As for the pilgrimage to St. James in Galicia,
it is a thing that is usually frequented all the
year, by such a number of people as you would
1940 scantly judge, among whom, divers of our
Englishmen be so holy that they will not stick
to bear them company. There, they say, lieth
the body of St. James the apostle; and there is
the cock that crowed when Peter denied
1945 Christ; some of the hair of Our Lady's head;
certain of the thorns of the crown of thorn;
the napkin that was about Christ's head in the
grave; certain drops of his blood; a piece of
the cross whereon he was crucified; and a
1950 number suchlike relics, which are honoured
and worshipped, as if they were God himself.

Then one of the chief pilgrimages is to a
place called S. Maria di Loreto, where within
is an old little brick room which they name to
1955 be the house Our Lady dwelt in; there is the
image of Our Lady all in gold and silver, the
house round about her beset with chalices of
gold and silver, which are oblations and offer-
ings of divers pilgrims that come in whole
1960 companies thither. And before her is a great
barred chest of iron wherein they throw money
to Our Lady, by whole goblets-full at once.
Within this little house there is an altar made
right before Our Lady, and there is said every
1965 day forty or fifty masses, whereat the people

1937. *St. James in Galicia*] St. James of Compostela,
Galicia, north-west Spain. This important pilgrimage shrine
claimed possession of an array of relics, chief among them
those of the apostle. In this case, of course, Munday is not a
visitor but a reporter of the accounts of others.

1941. *stick*] hesitate.

1953. *S. Maria di Loreto*] Another famous shrine, the
Holy House of the Blessed Virgin was said to have been trans-
ported by angels to Loreto, 15 miles south of Ancona over-
looking the Adriatic, and was the scene of numerous miracles.
Munday's description supports his claim to have visited the
shrine. See, e.g., the illustrations, tav. cxxix, between pp. 504
and 505, Vol. xxi of the *Enciclopedia italiana* (Rome, 1951).

will throng in great heaps, to get into the
house, for they think themselves happy if Our
Lady have once seen them. And all the church
is likewise hung with pictures, tapers, and wax
candles, which are the vows of the pilgrims to
Our Lady. I have heard of some who by the
counsel of their ghostly father have made
money of all their household stuff and have
come five or six hundred mile bare-foot and
bare-legged to give it all to Our Lady there:
meanwhile, the holy father hath had liberty
to play with the man's wife at etc. In all my
life I never saw a place more frequented with
people than this is daily, only for the admirable miracles that be done there. Some have
come thither for their eyesight: and when
they were there, they could see a little (as
they say) but they have come away stark
blind as they were before. A man came
thither, being grievously wounded on the sea
by his enemies: and after he had seen Our
Lady, he went to the hospital, and within a
quarter of a year after, at the furthest, the
chirurgeons had healed him. When he was
well again, he went and hung up his picture
in the church, that he was healed of his hurt
so soon as he looked upon Our Lady. Divers
have been brought thither in their beds, some
being sick, some wounded, or otherwise
diseased, and there they were set before Our
Lady, looking when she should say, 'Take up
thy bed and walk.' And because she could
not intend to speak to them, being troubled
with so many other suitors, they have been
carried to the hospital, and there they have

The miracles at
Our Lady of
Loreto.

1979–80. *admirable*] surprising.
1984. *blind . . . before*] with the implication that the
blindness is also that of ignorance.
1989. *chirurgeons*] surgeons.
1991. *that*] for that, because.

been either buried or cured; then such as recover their health must go set up their picture in the church, how that the very looking on Our Lady hath holpen them. Sundry
2005 other holy miracles done by Our Lady of Loreto I could rehearse, but they be so strange that no wise body will care for the hearing them; nevertheless, the Pope finds her a good sweet Lady of Loreto, for the pilgrimage to
2010 her increaseth his treasure, many thousands in a year.

The pilgrimage to Mount Falcon, to see St. Clare.

To Mount Falcon there is another pilgrimage, to see the body of St. Clare, which was buried I know not how many hundred years
2015 ago, and yet the body remaineth whole and sound, without any perishing of bone or skin. I have been at this place, and there in a long rich tabernacle of glass lieth, as they say, the same body of St. Clare: the hands and feet
2020 are to be seen, which I can aptly compare to the manner of the anatomy whereon the chirurgeons show every year their cunning; as for any flesh, there is none to be seen: but the bare bones, and the withered sinews, which
2025 being kept so bravely as that is, standing still in one place and never moved, I judge will continue a great while, and truly I take it to be some anatomy, as divers other have done

2003. *how that*] to show that, as a sign that.
2004. *holpen*] helped.
2012-13. *To . . . St. Clare*] This St. Clare, d. 1308, was abbess of a Montefalco convent. As Munday says below, her body reputedly remained uncorrupted and her cleft heart showed the Passion of Christ. Also noted for the liquefaction of her blood.
2019-27. *the hands . . . while*] Munday presumably means that the hands and feet look like dissected and poorly preserved parts of a body, withered by time so that little more than sinews remain; i.e. the whole thing is a cunning fraud, and not too successful at that. But the passage could be clearer.
2021, 2028. anatomy 2: anótomy 1. Dissected body.
2022. *cunning*] skill, knowledge.

that have seen it as well as I. The whole body (if there be any) is covered with a gown of black velvet, and the head covered, so that none can see it. There lieth by her a thing which, they say, was her heart, which being cleft asunder in the midst, the whole torment and passion of Christ was there in lively form to be seen. Then there is likewise by her a glass of her tears that she shed daily in remembrance of the bitter passion of Our Saviour: which tears, they say, are as fresh and sweet as they were on the first day.

There are a number other pilgrimages, as to Turin, to see the winding-sheet wherein Christ was laid, wherein, as they say, he hath left the perfect image of his body. This marvellous relic is never shown but once in fourteen year, and then to deceive the people with the greater authority, there must six cardinals come thither, and they must hold it abroad for everyone to see it, no other but they may presume to touch it. To Paris, to St. Denis in France, to Poitiers, and a number other places there be daily pilgrimages, to see a number like relics, as I have declared before: all these help to uphold the Pope, lest his kingdom should decay, and so his usurping title be clean worn out of memory.

The relics of St. Clare.

2030

2035

2040

Other pilgrimages to divers places.

2045

2050

2055

2042. *the winding-sheet*] the Holy Shroud, which bears the negative image of a human body. It was brought to Turin in 1578 from Chambéry by the Duke of Savoy, and is now exposed every thirty-three years.

2050-2. *To Paris . . . pilgrimages*] An important shrine in Paris was the Sainte Chapelle, housing relics of the Passion; the abbey of Saint-Denis-en-France, near Paris, was erected over the traditional site of the grave of the martyred St. Denis, d. 273?; and at Poitiers were the relics of St. Hilary, the tomb of St. Radegunda, and the impression of Christ's footprint in stone.

A new pilgrimage
risen up in Rome,
called Madonna di
Monte.

But now you shall hear of a new prop and
pillar wherewith the Pope is and will be marvellously strengthened, that is risen up little
2060 more than two year since: and at this new
holy place is wrought miracles of great
account. In the year of Our Lord 1580 about
the time of Easter, a certain poor man, one
that saw the simplicity of the people, how apt
2065 they were to believe every feigned invention,
he being a subtle and crafty fellow thought he
would come in with some device of his own
whereby he might get a great deal of money,
and beside, be canonized for a saint when he
2070 died.

He having concluded his practice with
divers other crafty companions as subtle as
himself, who should maintain all that he did
devise, feigned himself to dream in his bed
2075 that a vision appeared to him, willing him to
make clean his house, and to fall down and
reverence an old picture of Our Lady, which
stood in his house, when presently there
should be marvellous miracles accomplished
2080 there. His companions noised this abroad,
adding thereto such admirable protestation of
speech, as everyone that heard thereof conceived no small cause of wondering. This
aforesaid vision appeared to this man twice,
2085 all in one manner, by which time it was spread
abroad sufficiently: so that when it came the
third time, he did according as the voice bade

2057–8. *But now . . . pillar*] Munday claims to have heard
this story from one John Young who, we learn at ll. 2933–5
below, was a servant of Dr. Nicholas Morton in Rome. It
seems pointless to check its authenticity. Shrines of images of
the Blessed Virgin are numbered in the thousands in Italy
alone, over 200 of them honoured by papal crowning, so one
more or less is hardly remarkable.

2057. s.n. *Madonna di Monte*] Madonna of the Mount.

2071. *concluded*] determined.

2085. *all in one manner*] i.e. the vision was the same on
both occasions.

him, he arose, made clean his house, and fell
down and worshipped the picture of Our
Lady.   2090

His companions had, some of them, bound
up their legs, and went on crutches, some of
them feigned themselves to be blind, so that
they came no sooner before our Lady, but the   Miracles   very
lame recovered his legs, and the blind his 2095   strangely wrought.
sight. Then those few crutches that these
counterfeit fellows came withal were hung up
by the picture, and a number more, to make
the people believe so many lame folks were
healed, and likewise the report of the blind 2100
that received their sight, so that it was thought
a marvellous number were healed at this new-
found holy place.

Upon this, the resort of people thither was   Note the marvel-
truly incredible: gentlemen would come 2105   lous ignorance of
thither, and there hang up their velvet cloaks,   these people.
as an offering to Our Lady; gentlewomen
would come thither bare-foot and bare-legged,
and there hang up their velvet gowns, their
silk gowns, with other costly apparel, and go 2110
home again in their petticoats. As for the
money, jewels, and other treasure daily offered
there, it was most marvellous to see: for
therewith they have builded a very fair church
where this house stood. When they saw they 2115
were grown so rich, they made no account of
the old picture wherewith all the aforesaid
miracles were done, but they erected a costly
altar and thereon made a sumptuous new
picture of Our Lady, which the people do 2120
daily honour with marvellous resort. This is
faithfully affirmed by one John Young an
Englishman, who not long since came home
from Rome, and while he was there he well

2097. were 2: where 1.
2102. *marvellous*] surprising.
2104. *resort*] flocking together.

2125 noted the impudency of our Englishmen in
lauding and extolling this place and the
miracles there wrought: so that they as certainly believe in those miracles, as any
Christian doth in God.

2130   This John Young once questioned with one
of the English priests, why God did not as
well suffer such miracles to be done by his
son Jesus Christ, as altogether by Our Lady;
whereto the priest answered: 'Because among

A wise answer of
an Englishman.
2135 the heretics, they use little or no reverent
regard to Our Lady, but rather despise and
contemn her, therefore it is the will of God to
witness the power and heavenly authority she
hath by these and many such miracles, both
2140 here and in divers other places, rather than by
his son Christ.' Here may every good Christian
behold the horrible abuses used among this
satanical crew: their pilgrimages, their relics,
and all their crafty inventions; it is to be mar-
2145 velled that people will be so fond as to
believe.

As for the nails wherewith Our Saviour was
nailed on the cross, it is evidently registered
by learned writers that they were no more in
2150 number than three: yet I am sure in Rome
there is above a dozen nails, dispersed there
through divers churches, and they are not
ashamed to say that with every one of those
nails, Christ was nailed upon the cross.

Helena, the mother 2155 And for those three nails wherewith Christ
of Constantine the
emperor,   found
the cross of Christ
and gave the nails
to her son.
was nailed on the cross, Platina recordeth that
Queen Helena the mother of Constantine the
emperor, searching in the ground, by chance
found the cross whereon Christ was crucified

2137. *contemn her*] treat her with contempt.
2144. it is *2*: is *1*.
2145. *fond*] foolish.
2156. *Platina*] Bartholomaeus Sacchi de Platina, 1421–81,
Italian historian who compiled a history of the Popes. See
below.

and wherein the nails were still sticking, for 2160
which cause she builded there a temple in the
same place where she found the cross. All
these nails she gave to her son Constantine,
which he bestowed in this order. One of them
he caused to be fastened in the bridle of his 2165
horse, whereon he rode to the wars; another
he made to be wrought into his helmet, in the
place where he set his plume of feathers; and
the third he used to carry about with him, till
on a time he sailing on the *Hadriaticum* Sea, a 2170
tempest arose, so that the sea waxed very
rough, whereupon he cast 'the nail therein, to
assuage the rage thereof.

Thus have you heard what became of the
three nails wherewith Our Saviour was nailed 2175
on the cross: and yet it may be, that the nail
which Constantine threw into the sea (according as Ambrose doth likewise affirm it was)
took upon it the nature of a fish, and spawned
a great many of other nails, whereof those 2180
may be some that are held for such holy relics.
And because you shall not doubt whether this
be the opinion of Platina or no, I will here set
down the words according as they be in his
works: '*Platina in Vitis Pontificum, et in Vita* 2185
Silvestri Primi. Anno 339 ab urbe condita 1191.
Helena vero aedificato, eo in loco templo ubi
crucem repererat, abiens, clavos quibus Christi
corpus cruci affixum fuerat, secum ad filium
portat. Horum ille unum in frenos equi trans- 2190

2178. *Ambrose*] St. Ambrose, 339?-97. In his *De Obitu
Theodosii* he records the finding of the true cross and the
fate of the nails.
    2185-94. Platina . . . deiecit] I have checked Munday
against *Historia B. Platinae De Vitis Pontificum Romanorum*
(Cologne, 1611)—*P*. Translating Munday, 'Platina in the
Lives of the Popes, and in the Life of Sylvester I, A.D. 339
[316 in *P*.] . . .' From '*Helena vero aedificato*' Munday's
Latin, which he has already rendered into English in the
previous paragraph, is in agreement with *P*.
    2190. *frenos ed*: *froenos 1, 2*.

*tulit, quibus in proelio uteretur; alio pro cono
galeae utebatur; tertium in mare Hadriaticum
(ut ait Ambrosius) ad compescendas saevientis
maris procellas deiecit.'*

2195 Bishop Jewel, Bishop of Salisbury, preaching
at Paul's Cross in the beginning of Her Majesty's reign, took occasion by his text to en-
treat of a company of the popish relics, where
among he named the nails that nailed Christ
2200 on the cross, what a company the papists had
of them: two in one place, two in another,
and here one, and there another, so that he
could reckon to the number of seventeen that
they had. And then he told how at a visitation
2205 in his diocese, he found a nail at a gentleman's
house which the gentleman and divers of his
friends did worship and reverence for one of
the nails wherewith Christ was nailed on the
cross: from him he took it, and said, 'I have
2210 already reckoned seventeen in divers places,
and this is the eighteenth', which he pulled
forth, and showed it to all the people. 'This
is the merchandise of Rome: from reposing
any credit in them, or him that is the capital
2215 master of them, good Lord deliver us.'

A sermon of
Bishop Jewel, at
Paul's Cross.

2192. *galeae* 2: *galiae 1.*
2195-215. *Bishop Jewel . . . us*] Most of the surviving
sermons (as distinct from other works) of Bishop John Jewel,
1522-71, were published after Munday was writing. The
sermon to which Munday is referring does not appear in the
Certain Sermons of 1583, nor in the *Works* of 1609.
2211. eighteenth 2: eighteen *1.*

¶ The manner of the dissension in the English College between the Englishmen and the Welshmen, the banishment of the English-men out of Rome, and the Pope's sending for them again, with other matters worthy the 2220
reading.

CHAPTER 6

Having promised before in my book to re-hearse after what manner the Englishmen and Welshmen fell at variance in the College, I 2225
thought good to drive off the time no further but even here to set down how and in what sort it was. The Pope when he erected the College gave it the name of the English Col-lege, so that he supposed the Welsh and English 2230
to be all as one, in that they came all out of one country, allowing them his liberality jointly together. Now indeed there are sundry Welsh doctors in Rome who have been longest and of greatest familiarity with the Cardinal 2235
Morone, who was the Protector of the English College, to whom likewise he allowed greatest favour, so that emboldening themselves upon him, the Welshmen would be lords over the

2223–8. *Having . . . was*] This sentence seems to refer to the 1582 heading to Chapter Two. Munday seems originally to have intended plunging his narrative directly into the troubles of the College.

2228–9. *The . . . College*] The hospice only became a college, properly speaking, after Gregory XIII converted it into a seminary (1577–8; bull signed, canonically founding the College, 23 Apr. 1579, published 1580).

2233–6. *sundry . . . Morone*] Chief among these 'Welsh doctors' was Owen Lewis (see above, l. 377, note), whose influence with Morone and the Pope was probably responsible for his fellow Welshman Clenocke's appointment as rector in 1578. See A. Gasquet, *A History of the Venerable English College, Rome* (London, 1920), pp. 62–9. Giovanni Morone,

2240 Englishmen, and use them according as they
thought good.

Doctor Morris, being a Welshman, and
custos of the Hospital or College, would allow
his own countrymen greater pre-eminence
2245 than Englishmen, which indeed they began to
stomach, and would not esteem him for their
governor, but rather sought to have the Jesuits
to rule them, by whom they applied their
studies, and beside, they would be indifferent
2250 men on either part.

When I had been there a pretty while, I
know not how Doctor Morris conceived anger
against me, but he would not suffer me to
tarry any longer in the College. As for my
2255 fellow, his sincerity in their religion was such,
his natural disposition so agreeable with theirs,
and everything he did esteemed so well, that

1509–80, was Cardinal Protector of the English generally, as
well as official Protector of the College from 23 Apr. 1579.

2242–6. *Doctor Morris . . . stomach*] That it was Maurice
Clenocke's partial treatment of the seven Welsh students that
provoked the rebellion of the thirty-three English students is
borne out by contemporary accounts. The progress of the
rebellion is summarised by Gasquet, pp. 69 ff.

2246. *stomach*] resent.

2246. *esteem*] respect.

2247–9. *the Jesuits . . . studies*] see above, l. 924, note.

2249. *indifferent*] impartial.

2251 ff. *When I had . . .*] The following account of Munday's difficulties in the College and his personal role in the
rebellion is substantiated in part by a letter from Robert
Persons to William Goode, even though Persons does not
refer to Munday or Nowell by name. See *C.R.S. Miscellanea*,
ii (1906), 140–60 and esp. 155, the relevant area quoted by
Anthony Kenny, 'Antony Munday in Rome', p. 160, and
reproduced in the Appendix at the end of this text. Munday's
general outline of events, as distinct from his description of
his own part in them, is supported by several documents including Persons' letter to Goode, but principally by a first-
hand account sent to William Allen by one of the English
students involved in the affair, Allen's nephew Richard Haddock, dated 9 Mar. 1579, and printed in M. A. Tierney, ed.,
Dodd's Church History of England, Vol. ii (London, 1839),
Appendix, pp. cccl–ccclxi. Part of this is also reproduced in
the Appendix below. Where Munday's account seems to dis-
agree with Persons or Haddock, this will be noted.

Doctor Morris would suffer him willingly to
remain there; but he could not abide me in
any case. The scholars understanding this, as 2260
well they that bare me affection as they that
made least account of me, agreed to take my
part, saying that if Doctor Morris would put
every Englishman he thought good on, out,
in short time the College would be all Welsh- 2265
men: so they bade me stick to them, and if I
went away they would go away too.

Beside, they moved a certain speech
amongst themselves that if I were not received
into the College amongst them, and used in 2270
every respect according as they were, when I
returned into England, being knôwn to come
from Rome, I might be compelled to tell the
names of them that were there, and what conference I had among them, so that their 2275
parents and friends should be discovered, and
themselves be known against their coming
into England. To avoid therefore any such
doubt, until they had me sworn to priesthood:
they would keep me there, and then I should 2280
be as deep in any matter as they.

When I perceived the scope of their device,
I behaved myself more frowardly to Doctor
Morris than ever I did before: everything that
I heard of him I told unto the scholars, and 2285
tarried there dinner and supper in spite of his
nose. Whereupon he went and complained to

The Englishmen's
policy to keep me
there still.

2258-9. *Doctor Morris . . . there*] According to Persons's
letter to Goode, both were equally unwelcome. Munday is
less than fair to Nowell, both here and in the following pages.
2261. *bare*] bore.
2264. *thought good on*] felt inclined to.
2268. *moved . . . speech*] i.e. formed an agreement.
2281. *deep*] implicated (by long association).
2283. *frowardly*] perversely.
2286-7. *in . . . nose*] notwithstanding his opposition.
Tilley, S764.
2287-8. *he . . . Morone*] This visit to Morone, not mentioned in any of the documents, must have had its effect
since, according to Persons, the 'two youths' (Munday and

the Cardinal Morone how the scholars used no
regard to him, being their rector, but main-
2290 tained one lately come forth of England, both
to scorn at him, and to offer him too much
abuse.

This being come to the scholars' ear, and
how on the next day they must appear before
2295 the cardinal, they determined with themselves
all one resolute opinion, which was, that
Doctor Morris should be rector over them no
longer, but the Jesuits that were kept in the
house for the profit of their studies, and upon
2300 this they would all stand, denying any rectorship to Doctor Morris.

On the morrow they were sent for before
the Cardinal Morone, where they found
Doctor Morris and Doctor Lewis, they having
2305 made sound their tale before they came.
When they were come into the presence of
the cardinal and myself with them, these, or
the very like speeches he used unto us in Latin.

'You Englishmen, what meaneth this great
2310 disobedience, and uncivil behaviour you use

Nowell) 'had their answer from the Cardinal twice to depart
again'. See the Appendix below. Persons goes on to note that
the other students intervened, unsuccessfully, in the affair by
representing the case of Munday and Nowell to Morone, but
Munday is not explicit about this.

2302–03. *On . . . Morone*] one of several interviews between the students and Morone on the matter of grievances.
Almost certainly it was the interview of 28 Feb. 1579 (Haddock to Allen, in Tierney, p. ccclii), since those of 1 and 2
March Munday refers to later. Haddock confirms that Sherwin, whom Munday cites as the spokesman on this occasion,
was present at the interview of 28 February (though his list
of those present omits Munday), and Haddock's account of
this interview is in general conformity with Munday's. If this
is in fact the occasion Munday has in mind here, one has of
course to take his 'leave for a fortnight to lie in a . . . chamber'
granted subsequent to this interview (below, ll. 2423–4) as
time permitted rather than time spent there, for on 4 March,
less than one week after the interview, Munday left the College with the English students. There is no firm independent
evidence that Munday attended any of the interviews with

in your College? Master Doctor Morris, a man
of ancient time, and well esteemed here in the
city, being appointed to be your rector, and
to govern you in a good order, as a great while
he hath done: you, contrary to love and duty, 2315
behave yourselves ridiculously against him,
and neither respecting his credit and countenance, nor your own honesty, determine a
mutiny or tumult among yourselves. What is
the cause of this? You are sent for to manifest 2320
it, wherefore let me hear how you can excuse
this blame laid against you.'

Master Sherwin, who was executed with
Campion, being there esteemed a singular
scholar both for his eloquence, as also his 2325
learning, made answer for them all after this
manner.

'I trust, my gracious lord, by that time you
have heard the good cause we have to stir in
this matter, you will neither be offended at 2330
our proceeding nor displeased with us, the
cause tending to your own honour. It is not
unknown to you that the College or Hospital,
which by the gracious providence of our dear
Father the Pope's Holiness, we enjoy our 2335
abiding in at this present, hath been always
allowed such a sufficient stipend that one
should not be better than another, or excel
his fellow in common behaviour.

Master Sherwin's
answer to the car-
dinal on the behalf
of them all.

Morone, though Persons's letter to Goode suggests he may
have been present at the time the students put his and Nowell's
case to Morone, which must have been on 1 or 2 March.

2311–12. *a man . . . time*] Clenocke's date of birth is unknown, but as he received his B.C.L. in 1548 he must have
been at least fifty at this time.

2318. *honesty*] integrity.

2323. *Master Sherwin*] Ralph Sherwin, 1550–81, proto-
martyr of the English College, Rome; executed with Edmund
Campion and Alexander Briant on 1 Dec. 1581, and canonized
in 1970.

2338–9. *excel . . . behaviour*] have special privileges within
the community.

2340 'This most godly and holy-appointed estate, we both have been, and at this present are, content to obey; but when he that is the head shall fail in his duty, and urge an inconvenience among a quiet assembly, no marvel if the
2345 worm turn, being trodden upon, and we speak, being used with too much spite.

'Master Doctor Morris, whose age we reverence, and obey the title of his authority, dealing with us so unfriendly as he doth, we can
2350 hardly bear it, much less abide it. For where his office doth command him to deal both just and uprightly, and to use no partiality to either, for favour or alliance, he doth not only abuse the credit of his authority, but also mal-
2355 iciously deal with us, who have not so much as used an evil thought against him.

'When any Englishman cometh to the Hospital, if his learning be never so good, or his behaviour never so decent, except he be
2360 pleased, he shall not be entertained. But if a Welshman come, if he be never so vile a runagate, never so lewd a person, he cannot come so soon as he shall be welcome to him;
whether he have any learning or no, it maketh
2365 no matter, he is a Welshman, and he must be permitted. Then which of us hath the best gown, he must receive one that is all ragged and torn, and the new-come Welshman must have the best, because he is the *custos'*
2370 countryman: and many nights he must have the Welshmen in his chamber, where they must be merry at their good cheer, we glad to sit in our studies, and have an ill supper, because Master Doctor wasteth our commons

Doctor Morris kind to his own country-men.

2343-4. *urge ... among*] promote trouble within.
2359-60. *he*] The first 'he' refers to Clenocke.
2361. vile *ed*: vild *1, 2*.
2361-2. *runagate*] vagabond.
2374. *commons*] provisions.

upon his own countrymen, so that we must   2375
be content with a snatch and away. If there
be one bed better than another, the Welshman must have it, if there be any chamber
more handsome than another, the Welshman
must lodge there: in brief, the things of most   2380
account are the Welshmen's at command.

'This maketh many of us to wish ourselves
Welshmen, because we would gladly have so
good provision as they, and being countrymen
to our *custos*, we should be all used alike: 2385
excepting Master Doctor's nephew Morganus
Clenokus, he must be in his silk, though all
the rest go in a sack.

'To mitigate therefore all inconveniences,
that neither the Englishmen shall be despised,   2390
nor the Welshmen contemned, we desire that
the Jesuits in our College may receive the
rectorship; they labour for the profit of our
studies, and they being none of our nation or
country, will see equity used to either side: so   2395
our discord shall be quietly reformed, our
College a great deal better governed, ourselves
be encouraged to employ us more willingly to
our studies, and we shall jointly live together
in quietness. Where otherwise, our emulation   2400
shall be known at home in our country, how
we fall at variance here, and cannot agree: and
then shall our names be known, our parents
and friends openly discovered, then what the
end will be I leave to your honourable judge-   2405
ment.'

When the cardinal had heard this discourse
(being greatly affected to Doctor Morris,

> They desire the
> Jesuits for their
> governors.

> The cardinal so
> affected Doctor
> Morris that he
> should not leave
> his rectorship.

2386-7. *Morganus Clenokus*] Morgan Clenocke appears
as item 20 in the *Liber Ruber*.

2400. *emulation*] contention, rivalry.

2403. *then . . . known*] Elizabeth's secret service was
kept well informed in any case. In 1581, for example, a list
of the students in the College was received in London. *C.S.P.
Dom. 1581-90*, p. 15.

thorough his long abiding in Rome), he would
2410 not grant that he should be put from his
office, but bade them depart home again, and
show themselves obedient to the rector that
both the Pope and himself had appointed,
promising if he heard any more disturbance
2415 he would inform the Pope of it, which should
be but small to their profit.

So the cardinal not minded to hear them
any longer at that time, they departed home
to the College, greatly offended with them-
2420 selves that they had sped no better. And now
I must out of the College, there was no other
remedy; but yet thorough entreaty of the
Jesuits I had leave for a fortnight to lie in a
very sweet chamber, filled with old rusty iron;
2425 and all the trash of the house was put into that
chamber, being a vacant place, and serving for
no other purpose because it was next to the
common house of office, which aired the
chamber with so sweet a perfume, that but
2430 for name's sake of a chamber, and fear of
catching some disease, I had rather have lain
in the street amongst the beggars. Well,
froward as I was, so was I frowardly served,
which I think Doctor Morris did only to tame
2435 my youthfulness: for in this place, not long
before my coming to Rome, there lay one
tormented with a devil and so distraught of
his wits that they were fain to bind him there
in his bed.

Doctor Morris his 2440 So Doctor Morris, seeing I used myself
provision for my both careless of him and with little regard to
lodging. their religion, yet in such an order as they
could have small advantage of me, chambered
me there, where I think the devil was still left,

2428. *common . . . office*] lavatory.
2430. *name's . . . chamber*] it being at least a chamber in
name.
2431. lain *ed*: lien *1, 2*.

for every night there was such a coil among 2445
the old iron, such rattling and throwing down
the boards, that with the sweet smell came
out of the counting-house to my bed's head I
lay almost feared out of my wits, and almost
choked with that pleasant perfume; so that 2450
when I was laid in my bed, I durst not stir till
it was fair broad day, that I might perceive
every corner of my chamber, whether the
devil was there or no.

Every morning the priests and the scholars 2455
would come to visit me, giving me money to
send for my dinner and supper into the town,
because Doctor Morris mine old friend watched
them so near that I could not have so much as
a draught of wine in the house. Then I told 2460
them of the noise that was every night in my
chamber, when they verily believed that the
devil, having possessed a woman on the farther
side of the garden, did every night take up his
lodging in my chamber among the old iron. 2465

Wherefore one night, two of the priests
came to hallow my chamber, and brought
their holy water, and their holy candles, and
sprinkled about in every corner, giving me
also a pot of holy water to hang by my bed's 2470
side, that when I heard the stir again, I should
with the sprinkling brush throw it about the
chamber. And they gave me a pair of beads,
whereon I should say six paternosters, and six
Ave Marias, then they would warrant me the 2475
noise would be gone straightway.

The priests come with holy water to hallow my chamber.

Night came, and supping so well as I could,
with two *quatrines'* worth of leeks, one *quatrine* bestowed in *ricoct*, which is hard curds to

The manner of my supper at night.

2445. *coil*] turmoil.
2448. *counting-house*] properly, a private chamber where business is undertaken; here, of course, the lavatory.
2478. quatrines'] farthings'.
2479. ricoct] fresh creamy cheese; cf. mod. Italian *ricotta*.

2480 make cheese, a *bayock* in bread, and a *demi-boccale* of the *Vine Romanesco*, wherewith I supped so well as I might, albeit not so well as I would, yet a little thing serves to quench hunger. I had not been in my bed full an hour

2485 and an half, not daring to sleep for fear, nor keep my head out of the bed because of mine accustomed air, but then began the noise again, more vehement than the night before, the old iron was flung about the chamber, the

2490 boards that leaned against the wall fell down, and such a terrible coil there was, that I thought the house would have fallen on my head.

Then I put forth my hand to throw the

2495 holy water about, which did as much good as the thing is good of itself: which set me in such a chafe, that to make up the music among the old iron, I sent the pot and the holy water with as much force as I could. As

2500 for my beads, I was so impatient with myself that I gave them the place which they best deserved: and then I called to old Sir Robert, a Welsh priest who lay in a pretty chamber hard by, but before he would come the noise

2505 was indifferently pacified. For he coming with a candle in his hand, which he used to keep alight in his chamber, and being in haste, fell over a stone threshold that lay in his way

Sir Robert, a Welsh priest, coming to see what was the cause of the noise, fell over a threshold and brake his knee.

2480. bayock] baiocco; copper coin.
2480-1. *a* demi-boccale . . . Romanesco] a half-jug of Roman wine. The ironic effect of making the very ordinary sound exotic is typical of Munday. '*Vine*' is of course properly *vino*.
2483. *would*] i.e. would have liked.
2486-7. *mine accustomed air*] i.e. the smell.
2497. *chafe*] passion.
2501-2. *the place . . . deserved*] the lavatory receptacle?
2502. s.n. brake 2: berak *1*.
2503. *pretty*] fine.
2504. *would*] could.
2505. *indifferently*] one way or another.

so that he burst his knee very sore, and could
not light his candle again in the space of an   2510
hour, by which time all was quiet.

The fear I took at this noise brought me to
be very weak and sickly, so that I was very
unwilling to lie there any longer. But Doctor
Morris I thank him was so gentle to me, that   2515
he said, and if I liked not my lodging, 'go
hardly', quoth he, 'and lie in the street, for
that place is more meet for thee than any
room in the house.'

How I received these churlish words I leave   2520
to your judgements, but it sufficeth I gave
him my blessing, and if I could have gotten
him forth of Rome I would have bummed
him too.

On the next day, upon another complaint   2525
of Doctor Morris, the students were all sent
for again before the cardinal, who plainly said
unto them that except they would live in
quietness one with another (because there was
one Hugh Griffin, a Welshman of a hot nature,   2530
and he would many times fall together by the
ears with some of the scholars, that sometime
the blood ran about their ears), likewise, that
they should confess Doctor Morris for their
rightful rector, and be obedient to what he   2535
appointed, or else to get them away out of
Rome.

Well home they came again, incensed with
such anger and choler that they were now

2509. *sore*] severely.
2517. *hardly*] hardily.
2523. *bummed*] beaten.
2525. *the next day*] 1 March. The interviews of 1 and 2
March that Haddock refers to are clearly those Munday has
in mind in this and the following paragraph.
2530. *Hugh Griffin*] or Griffyth, item 35 in the *Liber
Ruber*. Haddock cites him (pp. cccliv and ccclx) as especially
quarrelsome. He was Owen Lewis's nephew (see the letter
from Allen to Lewis, in Tierney, p. ccclxvii).

2540 more disobedient than before, saying to Doctor Morris that they would never consent unto him, and therefore provided themselves to be packing out of Rome. Doctor Morris, thinking to bring them violently to his bow, 2545 informed the cardinal so severely against them that they were sent for the third time, when he commanded them to provide themselves, for they should stay no longer in the English Hospital, but banished them all from the city.

Doctor Morris beginneth to offer me gentleness.

2550 When they were come to the College, every man trussed up his needful things, determining on the next morning to depart; then came Doctor Morris to me and my fellow, willing us to stay, because the other would be gone, 2555 and he would stand our friend marvellously.

'Trust me no, sir,' quoth I, 'since you would not stand my friend when I was in great need, now I mean not to receive your courtesy when I care not for it; for since the students 2560 have stood my friends so much, and you mine enemy so greatly, I will bear a share in their travail however I speed. As for my fellow, since you have loved him all this while, love him now too if you please, and let him stay 2565 and do what you think best, for I have told you my mind.'

2544. *to his bow*] under his yoke.
2552. *the next morning*] This would be 3 March, but the English students left on 4 March. Munday seems to have overlooked a day. He also overlooks the fact that several of the students had unsuccessfully attempted to put their grievances to the Pope on 3 March. See Haddock, in Tierney, p. ccclvi.
2552–66. *then . . . mind*] cf. Persons's letter to Goode, p. 155 (and Appendix below): 'when all the English scholars were departed the seminary, signification was given them that they might have new places; but they would not, and retired themselves to the house of the scholars, meaning to depart Rome with them.' This suggests that Munday is quite misleading about Nowell's role here.
2554. *other*] others.
2555. *stand*] act as.
2562. *travail*] hardship.

Well, on the morrow morning we went our way, with bag and baggage, to an Englishman's house in the city, and as I remember, his name was Master Creed, where to make ready our dinner, every one took an office upon him, one to fetch milk, another to make ready rice for the pottage, some to make the fire, so that everyone was employed till our dinner was dispatched. Then they concluded to buy every man an ass, to carry his books and his clothes upon; as for money, there were gentlemen's sons of such credit amongst them that Doctor Morton, and the gentlemen in the city, would provide them with as good as five hundred crowns quickly. Within one hour and a half after dinner came Father Alfonso the Jesuit of the English College, whom the students had chosen and made suit to be their rector: he, I say, came running in such haste that he could hardly tell his tale because he was almost out of breath. But this was the sum of his news, that the Pope's Holiness had sent for them in all the haste, and they must delay no time, but come to him with all speed possible.

Then we went with him to the Pope's Palace, where coming into the Pope's chamber,

2570 *The Englishmen avoid the College.*

2575

2580

2585 *The scholars sent for before the Pope.*

2590

2570. *Master Creed*] John Creed according to Haddock.
2579–81. *Doctor ... quickly*] Haddock supports Munday as to the sum of money, but does not mention the part played by Nicholas Morton, *fl.* 1586.
2582–5. *Father ... rector*] Alfonso Agazzari was appointed rector of the College to replace Clenocke on 23 Apr. 1579, but according to Haddock and others, the students originally asked for either Dr. Morton or Dr. Bernard, both of them Englishmen.
2585. *he . . . came running*] Haddock mentions a priest but does not name him.
2589. *in . . . haste*] either 'in all haste' or, perhaps, 'in the general rush of events'.
2592–3. *Then ... Palace*] Munday's account is so close to Haddock's that there can be no doubt that he was present at the interview with Gregory XIII. In any case, Persons men-

and having everyone kissed his foot, we stayed
2595 to attend what was his pleasure. But before he
spake any word, with a dissembling and hypocritical countenance, he fell into tears, which
trickled down his white beard, and began in
Latin with these, or the very like words.
2600 'O you Englishmen, to whom my love is
such as I can no way utter, considering that
for me you have left your prince, which was
your duty, and come so far to me, which is
more than I can deserve, yet as I am your
2605 refuge when persecution dealeth straitly with
you in your country by reason of the heretical
religion there used, so will I be your bulwark
to defend you, your guide to protect you,
your Father to nourish you, and your friend
2610 with my heart-blood to do you any profit.'
Behold what deceits the Devil hath to accomplish his desire: tears, smooth speeches,
liberality, and a thousand means to make a
man careless of God, disobedient to his prince,
2615 and more, to violate utterly the faith of a subject. These tears that he shed, these words
that he spake, made divers of them say within
themselves, as one of them for example
presently to me said, 'O singular saint, whose
2620 life, love, and liberality may be a spectacle to
the whole world. Who would live in England,
under the government of so vile a Jezebel,
and may rest in safety under the perfect image
of Jesus? Who would not forsake father,
2625 mother, friends, goods, yea, and the life itself,
to have the bountiful blessing of such a provident Father?' The Pope recovering his health

The words of one
of the scholars.

---

tions that both the 'two youths' 'went to the Pope with' the
others (see Appendix below), while another letter dated 28
Mar. 1579 from Owen Lewis to Morone further confirms that
both Munday and Nowell were present. See Kenny, 'Antony
Munday in Rome', p. 159 and n. 3.
    2605. *straitly*] strictly.

again from his weeping, caused this devout
fellow to stay his talk, because he began again
as thus: 2630

'What is the cause that you will depart
from me, that have so well provided for you,
to thrust yourselves on the rock of your own
destruction?'

Then Master Sherwin began, and told him   2635
all the dealings of Doctor Morris toward them,
according as he had done before to the cardinal, and how they would have the Jesuits
for their governors, for the causes before mentioned. Upon these words the Pope started   2640
out of his chair.

'Why,' quoth he, 'I made the Hospital for   *The Pope supposed*
Englishmen, and for their sake I have given so *Englishmen and*
large exhibition, and not for the Welshmen.   *Welshmen all as*
Return to your College again, you shall have 2645 *one.*
what you will desire, and anything I have in
the world to do you good.'

Then he commanded one of the chief gentlemen of his. chamber to go with us, and to
certify the Pope's mind to Doctor Morris, and 2650
so giving us his benediction, we all went
merrily again to the College.

The gentleman gave Doctor Morris to understand he must be rector no longer; the Jesuit
named Father Alfonso, whom the scholars   2655
had chosen, must have his office; then were
the scholars glad, that they had gotten the
victory of the Welshmen.

On the morrow, the Pope sent four hundred   *The Pope's liberal-*
crowns to new reparation the house, to buy   2660 *ity.*
the students all needful things that they

2635. *Master Sherwin began*] Haddock is not specific as
to the students' spokesman on this occasion.
2638. *would*] wished to.
2644. *exhibition*] support—a sense still current.
2659-60. *the Pope . . . crowns*] Haddock does not mention this.
2660. *to new reparation*] towards the renovation of.

wanted, and the house must no longer be called a college, but a seminary.

2665 Then Cardinal Morone, because Doctor Morris should not lose all his dignity, caused the house to be parted, and so made both a seminary for the students, and an hospital for the entertainment of English pilgrims when they came, whereof Doctor Morris continued

2670 *custos*, by the Pope's appointment.

Thus was the strife ended, and myself and my fellow admitted by the Pope's own consent to be scholars there; but yet the sickness I got with lying in my former chamber hung

2675 still upon me, so that I was then removed to a very fair chamber, where the scholars every day would come and visit me until such time as I recovered my health again.

2662-3. *the house ... seminary*] It continued to be called the English College.

2664-70. *Then . . . appointment*] Clenocke's friends attempted to do for him precisely what Munday says Morone achieved, but contrary to what Munday says, the attempt was unsuccessful.

2666. *parted*] separated, divided.

2667. students 2: students 1.

2671-2. *myself . . . admitted*] This is supported by Persons's letter to Goode, p. 155 (see Appendix) as well as by obvious internal evidence in *E.R.L.* that Munday remained in Rome at least until Easter (19 April).

← Of the *Carne-vale* in Rome; the Pope's general cursing on Maundy Thursday; and the 2680 manner of the *Flagellante* that night.

CHAPTER 7

During the time of Shrove-tide there is in Rome kept a very great coil which they use to call the *Carne-vale*, which endureth the 2685 space of three or four days, all which time the Pope keepeth himself out of Rome, so great is the noise and hurly-burly. The gentlemen will attire themselves in divers forms of apparel, some like women, other like Turks, 2690 and every one almost in a contrary order of disguising; and either they be on horseback, or in coaches, none of them on foot, for the people that stand on the ground to see this pastime are in very great danger of their lives, 2695 by reason of the running of coaches and great horses, as never in all my life did I see the like stir. And all this is done where the courtesans

The burdella helps to maintain the Pope.

2679. Carne-vale] Munday splits the word—a common way of suggesting its possible origin: *carne vale*—flesh, farewell! See the *Encyclopaedia of Religion and Ethics*, iii (Edinburgh, 1910; edn. cited 1958), 225–9. The carnival is of course a Catholic rather than a merely Roman insitution, although it probably derives from the Roman saturnalia.

2680. *Maundy Thursday*] the Thursday (16 Apr. 1579) before Easter.

2681. Flagellante] Flagellant, flagellating.

2683. *Shrove-tide*] the three days before Lent—i.e. Sunday to Tuesday, 1–3 Mar. 1579.

2684. *coil*] fuss, ado.

2695. *pastime*] entertainment.

2698–704. *And . . . windows*] Things were similar in the early nineteenth century. See the illustration, top right, on tav. xxi, between pp. 104 and 105, Vol. ix of the *Enciclopedia italiana* (Rome 1949).

2698. s.n. *burdella*] brothel.

be, to show them delight and pastime, for
2700 they have coverlets laid out at their windows
whereon they stand leaning forth, to receive
divers devices of rosewater, and sweet odours
in their faces, which the gentlemen will throw
up to their windows.

2705 During this time every one weareth a disguised visor on his face so that no one knows
what or whence they be, and if anyone bear a
secret malice to another, he may then kill
him, and nobody will lay hands on him, for
2710 all this time they will obey no law. I saw a
brave Roman, who rode there very pleasant
in his coach, and suddenly came one who dis-
charged a pistol upon him, yet nobody made
any account either of the murderer or the
2715 slain gentleman: beside, there were divers
slain, both by villainy, and the horses or the
coaches, yet they continued on their pastime,
not making any regard of them.

The first day of their *Carne-vale*, the Jews
The Jews have 2720 in Rome cause an ensign to be placed at the
small pastime in Capitol, where likewise they appoint certain
this. But it is an wagers at their own costs; and then they run
order that they stark naked from *Porta populo* unto the
must do, whether Capitol for them, the which I judge above a
they will or no. 2725 mile in length. And all the way they gallop
their great horses after them, and carry goads
with sharp points of steel in them, wherewith
they will prick the Jews on the naked skin, if
so be they do not run faster than their horses

2702. *devices*] clever contrivances—but the sense is vague.
2702. *rosewater*] distillate of roses, used as perfume.
2711. *brave*] handsomely dressed.
2711. *pleasant*] merrily.
2719-39. *The . . . times*] The humiliating foot-race of
1579 to which Munday is such a graphic witness was repeated,
compulsorily, every year at carnival time from 1466 until
1668. Munday's syntax here is somewhat obscure, and one
has consciously to refer each 'they', 'them', and 'their' either
to the Romans or the Jews.
2720. *ensign*] presumably a banner of some kind.

gallop, so that you shall see some of their 2730
backs all on gore blood. Then he that is foremost, and soonest cometh to the Capitol, he
is set on a horse back without any saddle, one
going before him carrying the ensign: but
then you shall see a hundred boys, who have 2735
provided a number of oranges, they will so
pelt the poor Jew, that before he can get up
to the Capitol, he will be beaten beside his
horse four or five times.

The next day there are certain of the 2740
Christians that run naked likewise, but nobody
pursueth them, either with horse or coach,
and the wager they run for, the Jews must pay
likewise. Then the buffle and the ass runneth,
but it is unpossible for me to tell all the 2745
knavery used about this: and therefore thus
much shall suffice of the *Carne-vale*, letting
you understand, that they who were most
knavishly disposed in this sport, on Ash
Wednesday came to take ashes in such meek 2750
order, as though it had never been they.

On Maundy Thursday, the Pope cometh
into his gallery over St. Peter's, sitting in the
chair wherewith he is carried on men's
shoulders, and there he hath a great painted 2755
holy candle in his hand burning, whenas a
cardinal on each side of him, the one in Latin,
the other in Italian, singeth the Pope's general
malediction.

There he curseth the Turk, and Her Majesty, 2760   The Pope's curses
our most gracious Princess and governess,   will return to him-
affirming her to be far worse than the Turk,   self.
or the cruellest tyrant that is. He curseth

2738-9. *beside his horse*] Munday may mean that he was
beaten into a position beside his horse, or that he was beaten
as well as his horse.

2744. *buffle*] form of the word *buffalo*; ox.

2759. *malediction*] cursing. The following people or
groups are outside the Church and are therefore anathema in
terms of the teaching of the times.

likewise all Calvinians, Lutherans, Zwinglians,
2765 and all that are not according to his disposition. When he hath cursed all that he can,
saying amen, he letteth the candle fall: whenas
the people will scamble for it, and every one
catch a little piece if they can, yea, our
2770 Englishmen will be as busy as the best; and
one of them chanced to get a piece of the wax
of the candle, whereof he made such a bragging
when he came to the College, as you will not
think that he had got a piece of the candle
2775 wherewith the Queen of England was cursed,
and that he would keep it so long as he lived.

The same night a number of the basest
people and most wicked livers that be amongst
the people gather themselves together in com-
2780 panies, as the Company of the Holy Ghost,
the Company of Charity, the Company of
Death, and suchlike, every company their
crucifix before them, their singers following
them, on either side a number of burning
2785 torches, and thus they go all whipping themselves.

First they go up into the Pope's Palace, and
then down into St. Peter's Church, which is
all adorned with a number of wax lights; and
2790 there on the top of an altar standeth a couple
of cardinals, who showeth them the holy
handkercher, or *Vultus sanctus* (which indeed
is nothing but a lively painted picture, over-
shadowed with a couple of fine lawns, and

Was this the part of a subject?

The manner of the Flagellante.

A fine piece of knavery, to deceive the people.

2764. *Calvinians*] Calvinists. *O.E.D.* cites this as the first example of the sb.
2768. *scamble*] obs. form of *scramble*.
2779–86. *The . . . themselves*] Munday is referring to 'associations of *Disciplinati*, common especially in Italy from *c.* 1350 until the end of the sixteenth century. These con-fraternities were under the control of the Church'. *New Catholic Encyclopedia* (New York, 1967), v. 955.
2792. Vultus sanctus] the veronica referred to, along with the spearhead, at ll. 1246–52 above.
2794. *lawns*] pieces of linen.

nobody must desire to see it uncovered, 2795
because they say nobody is able to endure the
brightness of the face; a number have seen it,
and have been the worse a great while after),
and all the while that both this, and the spearhead, is shown they will whip themselves 2800
before them very grievously, and give a general clamour thorough the church: '*Misericordia, misericordia, tu autem Domine miser-
ere nobis*'; and in this order they continue
almost the whole night. This is the glory of 2805
the Pope, the blindness of the people, and the
great folly of our Englishmen, to bring themselves within the compass of such wicked order
of life.

God continue his loving and fatherly count- 2810
enance over England; bless and preserve Her
Majesty, and her Honourable Council; and
exercise us all in fear to him, obedience to
her, and faithful and continual love to our
neighbours. Amen. 2815

2802-04. Misericordia . . . nobis] 'Mercy, mercy, Lord
have mercy on us.'

A true report of the Christian suffering and merciless maryrdom of one Richard Atkins, Englishman, at Rome: who for the truth of the gospel, to the great terror of all 2820 the beholders endured the extremity of the torment and cruel agony of death, in the year of Our Lord 1581.

CHAPTER 8

About the time of midsummer in the year 2825 1581 one Richard Atkins, a Hertfordshire man, came to Rome, and having found the English College he knocked at the door, when-as divers of the students came to welcome him, knowing that he was an Englishman. 2830 Among other talk, they willed him to go to the Hospital, and there to receive his meat and lodging, according as the order was appointed; whereto he answered, 'I come not, my countrymen, to any such intent as you 2835 judge, but I come lovingly, to rebuke the great misorder of your lives, which I grieve to hear, and pity to behold. I come likewise to let your proud Antichrist understand that he doth offend the heavenly majesty, rob God of 2840 his honour, and poisoneth the whole world with his abominable blasphemies, making them homage stocks and stones, and that

His counsel to his countrymen.

2816-22. *A true . . . 1581*] Munday's is one of only two printed accounts of Atkins's execution. The other is the anonymous *Copy of a Double Letter . . . containing . . . the cause, and manner of the death, of one Richard Atkins, executed by fire in Rome, the second of August 1581*. This, a Catholic report, is much fuller than Munday's independent account but omits one or two details Munday gives. A few instances where Munday's report adds to or contradicts it will be noted.

2831. *the Hospital*] i.e. the Hospice, that part of the College still reserved for English visitors.

2842-3. *that filthy sacrament*] of the Eucharist. *The Copy* claims that Atkins believed in none of the sacraments, that he

filthy sacrament, which is nothing else but a
foolish idol.'

When they heard these words, one Hugh   2845
Griffin, a Welshman and a student in the
College, caused him to be put in the Inquisition, where how they examined him, and how
he answered them, I know not, but after certain days he was set at liberty again.   2850

And one day going in the street he met a   1.
priest carrying the sacrament, which offend-   His attempt to
ing his conscience to see the people so crouch   smite down the
and kneel to it, he caught at it to have thrown   sacrament.
it down, that all the people might see what   2855
they worshipped. But missing his purpose,
and being judged by the people that he did
catch at the holiness that (they say) cometh
from the sacrament upon mere devotion, he
was let pass, and nothing said to him.   2860

Few days after, he came to St. Peter's   2.
Church, where divers gentlemen and other   His attempt in St.
were hearing mass, and the priest being at   Peter's Church.
the elevation: he using no reverence, stepped
amongst the people to the altar, and threw   2865
down the chalice with the wine, striving
likewise to have pulled the cake out of the
priest's hands. For which, divers rose up and
beat him with their fists, and one drew his
rapier and would have slain him; so that, in   2870

---

was no longer of the English Church, and that he had previously criticized Elizabeth and spent some time in English
prisons.

2845-6. *Hugh Griffin*] not cited in *The Copy*.

2846-8. *a student . . . Inquisition*] He was sent first to a
hospital 'till his fever was past', according to *The Copy*, and
only later, after the 'outrages', to the Inquisition.

2851-60 *And . . . him*] *The Copy* omits this incident.

2851. s.n. *1.*] This and subsequent numbers refer to the
woodcut illustration.

2863-4. *being at the elevation*] i.e. lifting the consecrated
elements.

2867. *cake*] consecrated host.

brief, he was carried to prison, where he was examined wherefore he committed such an heinous offence: whereto he answered that he came purposely for that intent, to rebuke the 2875 Pope's wickedness and their idolatry. Upon this he was condemned to be burned, which sentence he said he was right willing to suffer, and the rather, because the sum of his offence pertained to the glory of God.

Our Englishmen's 2880 During the time he remained in prison labouring to him, and his persuading them. sundry Englishmen came unto him, willing him to be sorry for that he had done, and to recant from his damnable opinion, but all the means they used were in vain; he confuted 2885 their dealings by divers places of scripture, and willéd them to be sorry for their wickedness while God did permit them time, else they were in danger of everlasting damnation: these words made the Englishmen depart, for 2890 they could not abide to hear them.

3. His going to execution. Within a while after he was set upon an ass without any saddle, he being from the middle upward naked, having some English priests with him, who talked to him; but he regarded 2895 them not, but spake to the people in so good language as he could, and told them they were in a wrong way and therefore willed them for Christ's cause to have regard to the saving of their souls.

2900 All the way as he went, there were four did nothing else but thrust at his naked body with burning torches: whereat he neither moved nor shrunk one jot, but with a cheerful count-

O marvellous patience, and Christian boldness. enance laboured still to persuade the people,

2871. *to prison*] to the Inquisition, according to *The Copy*.

2874-5. *to . . . idolatry*] and to suffer martyrdom, either here or in Turkey, according to *The Copy*.

2884-5. *he confuted . . . scripture*] according to *The Copy* he was barely literate.

2885. *dealings*] conduct, way of life.

often bending his body to meet the torches as 2905
they were thrust at him, and would take them
in his own hand, and hold them burning still
upon his body, whereat the people not a little
wondered. Thus he continued almost the
space of half a mile till he came before St. 2910
Peter's where the place of execution was.
When he was come to the place of execution,   4.
there they had made a device, not to make
the fire about him, but to burn his legs first,
which they did, he not dismaying any whit, 2915
but suffered all marvellous cheerfully, which
moved the people to such a quandary as was
not in Rome many a day. Then they offered
him a cross and willed him to embrace it, in   They offered him
token that he died a Christian: but he put it 2920   a cross to embrace.
away with his hand, telling them that they
were evil men to trouble him with such paltry,
when he was preparing himself to God, whom
he beheld in majesty and mercy, ready to
receive him into the eternal rest. They seeing 2925
him still in that mind, departed, saying, 'Let
us go, and leave him to the Devil, whom he
serves.' Thus ended this faithful soldier and
martyr of Christ, who is no doubt in glory
with his Master, whereto God grant us all to 2930
come. Amen.

   This is faithfully avouched by the aforesaid John Young, who was at that time and
a good while after in Rome, in service with
Master Doctor Morton, who seeing the martyr- 2935
dom of this man, when he came home to his
house, in the presence of Master Smithson,

   2905–09. *often . . . wondered*] *The Copy* claims he shrunk
from the torches in pain and called, 'kill me at a stroke'.
   2916. *suffered . . . cheerfully*] Such was his torment that
he tried to strangle himself with the binding chains, according
to *The Copy*.
   2922. *paltry*] trash.
   2927. *leave . . . Devil*] *The Copy* mentions that he signalled
at the end his repentance and recantation.

Master Creed, and the said John Young his
servant, spake as followeth.

2940 'Surely, this fellow was marvellous obstinate;
he nothing regarded the good counsel was
used to him, nor never shrunk all the way
when the torches were thrust at his naked
body. Beside, at the place of execution he did
2945 not faint or cry one jot in the fire, albeit they
tormented him very cruelly and burned him
by degrees, as his legs first, to put him to the
greater pain; yet all this he did but smile at.
Doubtless, but that the word of God can be
2950 but true, else we might judge this fellow to be
of God: for who could have suffered so much
pain as he did? But truly I believe the Devil
was in him.'

Behold, good reader, how they doubt among
2955 themselves, and because they will not speak
against their master the Pope, they infer the
mighty power of God upon the Devil; but he
no doubt one day will scatter the chaff, and
gather his chosen corn into his garner. That
2960 we may be of this good corn, let us defy the
Pope, his hellish abominations, continue in
our duty to God, faithful obedience to Her
Majesty, and unity among us all as brethren:
and then no doubt but we shall enter the land
2965 of the living, to our eternal comfort and con-
solation.

FINIS. Anthony Munday

The picture herein adjoined doth lively
decipher the order of the martyrdom of the
2970 aforesaid Richard Atkins, at Rome.

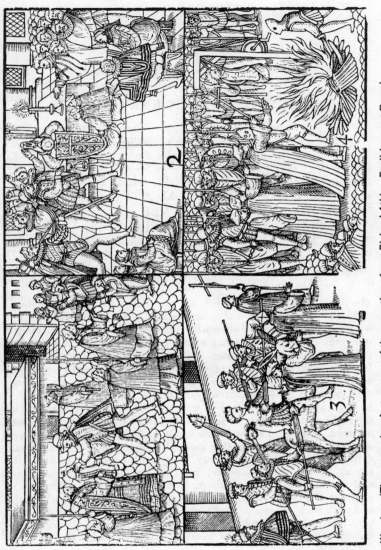

Woodcut, 'The true and perfect manner of the execution of one *Richard Atkins*, Englishman at Rome'.

APPENDIX

FROM TWO CONTEMPORARY LETTERS

1. *Richard Haddock to William Allen*

(Haddock's letter, written on 9 March 1579, is particularly relevant to Chapter Six of *E.R.L.*, which it generally substantiates. It is reproduced in M. A. Tierney, ed., *Dodd's Church History of England*, Vol. ii (London, 1839), Appendix, pp. cccl-ccclxi. In the following extract from Tierney, Haddock describes the English students' departure from the College, their preparations for leaving Rome, and their audience with Gregory XIII.)

The next day [4 Mar. 1579] in the morning, we departed the house unto one John Creed's, our countryman's, house, all together; where we all dined that day; wherewith were so amazed our adversaries, that they could not tell what to do. Those that hated us were glad; those that had any compassion at all were afraid, and seemed sorrowful; but more for themselves, than for us. They thought we should never have gone so far, when they began the tragedy; for, in very deed, we were fully appointed of departing, thirty-three in company; having nothing in the world to bear our charges. Yet no man, from the highest to the lowest, was any thing discomforted. For there was no need. You would have blessed you, to have seen the affection of our friends towards us in that case. Mr. Archdeacon [Owen Lewis] denied to give one penny to any. The Jesuits began to beg in pulpits for us, being Ash-Wednesday, and the first day of preaching; but without naming us. Our fathers, in our house, began to beg for us amongst their company, as of the general, provincial, and others; and with such diligence, that you will scarce believe what had been very like to have been had, for our viaticum; besides all begging by the way, which is much for pilgrims. And at Siena is the rector of the Jesuits, he who was our father, the last summer, whom Mr. Licentiate Martin knoweth, father John Paul; where we had fifty crowns appointed for us to have taken by the way. Our father Ferdinando was almost mad for us, and begged for us of the fathers of the Casa (which needed not) to appoint of a great sum for us: insomuch that I think, we should have brought you home four or five hundred crowns. For we had been like to have no less than a thousand crowns. For my lords prepared for us a hundred crowns,—

Italians, that heard of our case, and took the matter wonderfully heinously, that we should be so dealt with; protesting that they would go unto the pope for us, and help us, that we might have justice, and be heard. But God provided for us otherways. The Jesuits were out of their wits almost for us: insomuch that they wept, many of them, and desired that we should not come, and take leave of them; for they could not find in their hearts to take leave with us. Father General, and all the company, would have gone unto the pope for us, but that he had been slandered by Mr. Archdeacon's railing, being warned by their friends secretly; yet, by some of their friends of great account, they knew they would be working that, all the world knew not of. The answer unto our supplication unto the pope was, that we should come kiss his foot before we departed; which we were glad of wonderfully, and proposed that, before we should depart; meaning to defer it a day or two, for fear we should seem importunate: in the mean time, thinking to make friends unto the cardinal, some other cardinals of his best friends, and the ambassadors of Spain and Portugal, to signify unto him, that we departed not of any obstinancy or misliking, but only moved by our conscience: meaning for ever to remain in due obedience unto the see apostolic, and all our superiors. Which when we were thinking upon, there came a messenger of the pope's unto the hospital, to call us out of hand unto the pope; but being answered by the father, that we were departed, he requested that we might be certified; which the father did not slacken to do; and, finding one in the streets, by him called the rest, and to go unto the pope straightly: who going unto the house where we dined, and finding sixteen or seventeen there, went immediately unto the palace, not knowing what was fore-warned. They, kissing his holiness's foot, began to request his holi-ness's blessing, before they departed. And here the most blessed father in the world, whereas they were in doubt what he would do, began to burst into tears, and asked,—'and are you then gone out of the seminary?' They answered, 'yea:' and he said,—'why would you go out unknown to me, or not telling me before?' They answered, that the cardinal had twice in his name commanded us. And [he] asked, whither they meant to go? And they told him, some into England, those that were fit, being priests, and many others divines. 'Why,' said he, 'be these so young, divines?' (meaning by Christopher Owen, Pitts, and Gratley). And they answered, 'yea:' and all the rest philosophers and logicians alike. Said he, 'why would you depart from Rome, where good manners, and religion, and learning is to be gotten? You must not in any wise depart; but you shall go home again, and have what you desire.' Which when they heard him so heartily speak, they all fell a-weeping very fast, that they were heard sob, and could scarce speak unto him, and he unto them. And he asked them where they dined? They told him where; and how we prepared our dinner with our own hands; and that others of the company were going about the town, providing for our meat and viaticum to depart with. And he said, 'you should have come to me first for your viaticum. But go home again, and give me the names of some of your countrymen; and you shall have one of them: for this you shall have no longer.' And so kissing his foot again, with such joy that is not possible to express, they departed. And as they were going, he asked, if they would not one of his chamberlains to go home with them? And they said, 'yes;' because they were not sure that Mr. Maurice would credit them: and so he rung his bell for one of them, whom he sent with them unto our house. Which when the rest knew, it was such a common joy, and so strange a thing, that we wondered all at it.

2. *Robert Persons to William Goode*

(In the following extract from a long letter describing the troubles in the English College in Rome, Persons clearly refers to Munday and Nowell, though without naming them. See *C.R.S. Miscellanea*, ii (1906), 140–60, and esp. 155. The spelling has been modernized.)

In this act one thing fell out prettily. There were two youths sent and arrived at Rome a month before this act fell out, and by no means could be admitted into the seminary, but had their answer from the cardinal twice to depart again. And albeit [it] was said that Dr. Allen had recommended them, yet there was answer made, *Si Alanus misit, Alanus provideat eis*, which moved much Englishmen, for they doubted much what should become of those who after should be from that place sent by him, and if his recommendation served not, who must be the fountain to serve the seminary here, then was all hope past. Whereupon the scholars themselves went to the cardinal requesting him that, seeing these youths were like to perish in the streets for want, that his Grace would be content to give them leave to divide their portion with them, and so to save them from perishing. This was Mr Martin Array his request with others, wherewith the cardinal seemed somewhat moved, but yet commanded them to shift for themselves for the present, notwithstanding he would talk with his Holiness about them: and after having talked, I think Mr Morris brought a new commandment for them to depart, for that they could not be received. But within two days after, when all the English scholars were departed the seminary, signification was given them that they might have new places; but they would not, and retired themselves to the house of the scholars, meaning to depart Rome with them, and so went to the Pope with them, and there hence the Pope sent them into the seminary with the rest, and by this mean they got their interest as the others.

INDEX TO ANNOTATIONS

Arabic numerals refer to line-numbers, lower-case roman numerals
to page numbers, in the Introduction

110   INDEX